Writing the Critical Essay

CLONING

An OPPOSING VIEWPOINTS® Guide

William Dudley, *Book Editor*

Bruce Glassman, *Vice President*
Bonnie Szumski, *Publisher, Series Editor*
Helen Cothran, *Managing Editor*

OPPOSING
VIEWPOINTS®
SERIES

GREENHAVEN PRESS
An imprint of Thomson Gale, a part of The Thomson Corporation

THOMSON
✦
GALE

Detroit • New York • San Francisco • San Diego • New Haven, Conn. • Waterville, Maine • London • Munich

For more information, contact
Greenhaven Press
27500 Drake Rd.
Farmington Hills, MI 48331-3535
Or you can visit our Internet site at http://www.gale.com

06-07

06-07GG 21.09

LIBRARY OF CONGRESS CATALOGING-IN-PUBLICATION DATA

Cloning / William Dudley, book editor.
   p. cm. — (Writing the critical essay)
  Includes bibliographical references and index.
  ISBN 0-7377-3196-6 (lib : alk. paper)
  1. Cloning—Social aspects. 2. Cloning—Moral and ethical aspects. 3. Essay—Authorship. 4. Rhetoric. I. Dudley, William, 1964– . II. Series.
  QH442.2.C5646 2006
  176—dc22

                                           2005052569

Printed in the United States of America

CONTENTS

Section Two: Model Essays and Writing Exercises

Section Three: Supporting Research Material

Examining the state of writing and how it is taught in the United States was the official purpose of the National Commission on Writing in America's Schools and Colleges. The commission, made up of teachers, school administrators, business leaders, and college and university presidents, released its first report in 2003. "Despite the best efforts of many educators," commissioners argued, "writing has not received the full attention it deserves." Among the findings of the commission was that most fourth-grade students spent less than three hours a week writing, that three-quarters of high school seniors never receive a writing assignment in their history or social studies classes, and that more than 50 percent of first-year students in college have problems writing error-free papers. The commission called for a "cultural sea change" that would increase the emphasis on writing for both elementary and secondary schools. These conclusions have made some educators realize that writing must be emphasized in the curriculum. As colleges are demanding an ever-higher level of writing proficiency from incoming students, schools must respond by making students more competent writers. In response to these concerns, the SAT, an influential standardized test used for college admissions, required an essay for the first time in 2005.

Books in the Writing the Critical Essay: An Opposing Viewpoints Guide series use the patented Opposing Viewpoints format to help students learn to organize ideas and arguments and to write essays using common critical writing techniques. Each book in the series focuses on a particular type of essay writing—including expository, persuasive, descriptive, and narrative—that students learn while being taught both the five-paragraph essay as well as longer pieces of writing that have an opinionated focus. These guides include everything necessary to help students research, outline, draft, edit, and ultimately write successful essays across the curriculum, including essays for the SAT.

Using Opposing Viewpoints

This series is inspired by and builds upon Greenhaven Press's acclaimed Opposing Viewpoints series. As in the parent series, each book in the Writing the Critical Essay series focuses on a timely and controversial social issue that provides lots of opportunities for creating thought-provoking essays. The first section of each volume begins with a brief introductory essay that provides context for the opposing viewpoints that follow. These articles are chosen for their accessibility and clearly stated views. The thesis of each article is made explicit in the article's title and is accentuated by its pairing with an opposing or alternative view. These essays are both models of persuasive writing techniques and valuable research material that students can mine to write their own informed essays. Guided reading and discussion questions help lead students to key ideas and writing techniques presented in the selections.

The second section of each book begins with a preface discussing the format of the essays and examining characteristics of the featured essay type. Model five-paragraph and longer essays then demonstrate that essay type. The essays are annotated so that key writing elements and techniques are pointed out to the student. Sequential, step-by-step exercises help students construct and refine thesis statements; organize material into outlines; analyze and try out writing techniques; write transitions, introductions, and conclusions; and incorporate quotations and other researched material. Ultimately, students construct their own compositions using the designated essay type.

The third section of each volume provides additional research material and writing prompts to help the student. Additional facts about the topic of the book serve as a convenient source of supporting material for essays. Other features help students go beyond the book for their research. Like other Greenhaven Press books, each book in the Writing the Critical Essay series includes bibliographic listings of relevant periodical articles, books, Web sites, and organizations to contact.

Writing the Critical Essay: An Opposing Viewpoints Guide will help students master essay techniques that can be used in any discipline.

Background to Controversy: Basic Questions About Cloning

A clone is a genetic duplicate of a living thing. Genes are the chemical instructions found in every cell. They control what cells do and determine an organism's physical traits (size, skin color, eye color, etc.). You share some physical traits with your father and other traits with your mother because each parent contributed half of the genes found in your cells. A clone, such as Dolly, the sheep made famous during the 1990s, does not receive half of her genes from a mother and half from a father. Dolly's genes instead all came from one udder cell of one sheep.

In addition to sheep, scientists have successfully created clones of frogs, cows, cats, mice, and other animals. However, most of the public fascination, fear, and controversy around cloning has focused on humans. There are two fundamental questions about human cloning that have yet to be settled: *Can* it be done? and *should* it be done? The first is a question of science. The second is a question of morality—of right and wrong.

Can Humans Be Cloned?

The central scientific puzzle in cloning is how to get an adult cell to begin the process of division and development that culminates in a new organism. In 1964 scientists successfully did this with a frog cell. They did so by taking the genetic nucleus from an adult frog cell and injecting it into an egg whose nucleus had been removed. The egg, with its new genetic nucleus, developed into a new cloned frog. These experiments caused some people to speculate on the possibility that humans may be cloned

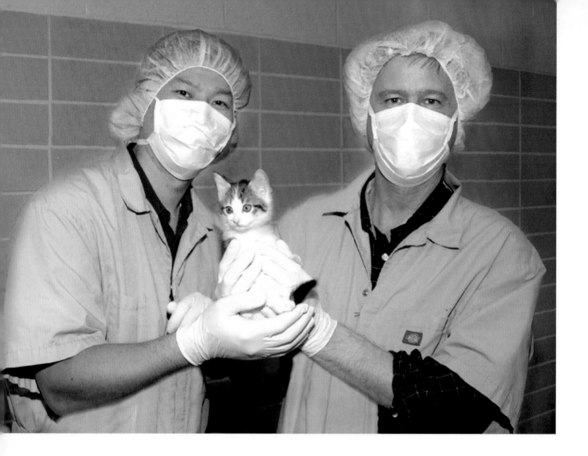

In recent years, researchers have cloned various animals, including this cat named Carbon Copy, the first cat ever cloned.

as well. But frogs are relatively simple animals compared with humans and other mammals. For many years most scientists believed that cloning was impossible for more complex animals. The cloning of Dolly the sheep in 1996 was hailed as a major and even shocking breakthrough because she was the first successfully cloned mammal. Scientists not only created a sheep embryo by combining the genetic nucleus of an adult cell with an egg cell, but they then also successfully implanted the embryo into the uterus of another sheep, where it developed into a seemingly healthy and normal lamb.

Could this procedure be used to create a healthy cloned human baby? On December 27, 2002, the organization Clonaid announced the birth of "Eve." It claimed the baby was the world's first human clone, but many scientists expressed skepticism about the organization's announcement. They noted that transferring genetic material to egg cells, getting the egg cells to start dividing in the lab, and implanting embryos in wombs were all technically difficult and delicate procedures that need to be done flawlessly in order to succeed. Even Dolly's successful birth in 1996 was the one successful cloning result out of 277 attempts; most cloning experiments with animals have had roughly similar success rates, if they were successful at all. In many animal cloning experiments, problems with cloning resulted in malformed fetuses and miscarriages. Concerns about Clonaid's credibility were also heightened due to the organization's affiliation with the

MARCH 10, 1997 $2.95

TIME

FICTION BONUS:
"CLONE ON THE RANGE"
BY DOUGLAS COUPLAND

Will There Ever Be Another You?

A SPECIAL REPORT ON CLONING

The cloning of Dolly the sheep raised the possibility of human cloning.

Raelians, a religious sect that believes human life is the creation of extraterrestrials. Years later, Clonaid's claim that it had produced a human clone has yet to be independently confirmed by genetic testing of the baby and genetic parent. However, many observers believe that cloning experiments may be happening in secret and that the birth of a human clone at some point is inevitable.

Ethical Questions

Should news of a confirmed birth of a human clone be celebrated or feared? Some people argue that cloning should be seen as just another method of assisted reproduction for individuals who desire to have children, similar to in vitro fertilization. Other hypothetical situations have been raised by cloning advocates. A married cou-

In 2000 Clonaid recruited these women to serve as surrogate mothers for cloned babies.

ple with known risks of passing on a genetic disorder to their children may turn to cloning to prevent such a thing. A woman who lost a baby to a car accident may wish for the opportunity to bring the infant back again. Promoters of cloning argue that a cloned human would be indistinguishable from other humans and thus will be treated with the same rights—there is no reason why clones would automatically become second-class citizens under the law.

But many people in America and other countries remain deeply suspicious of human cloning, believing it to be unnatural and even unholy. Many people oppose cloning because of religious teachings that hold the sexual creation of new human beings to be a gift from God that should not be tampered with. "Cloning risks being the tragic parody of God's omnipotence," proclaimed the Roman Catholic Church in 1997. In other words, human cloning would be a case of humans attempting to play God, and doing poorly. Other critics focus on the physical and mental health of possible clones. They argue

Roman Catholic bishops take part in a 1997 council at the Vatican. The church is among several religious institutions that oppose cloning.

that human clones would be at higher risk for physical disorders (as seen in many animal cloning experiments) and may also suffer a sense of deprivation and dehumanization because they know that they are not genetically unique. For these and other reasons, many nations of the world have outlawed cloning, and the U.S. government has debated its own cloning ban.

Answering the Questions

Whether human cloning *can* be done is a scientific and technical question that may be resolved with a few more years of research. But the question of whether human cloning *should* be done will not be answered so definitively. Even if a human clone is triumphantly presented to the world, the ethical, religious, and moral debates about the wisdom of pursuing this technology are sure to continue.

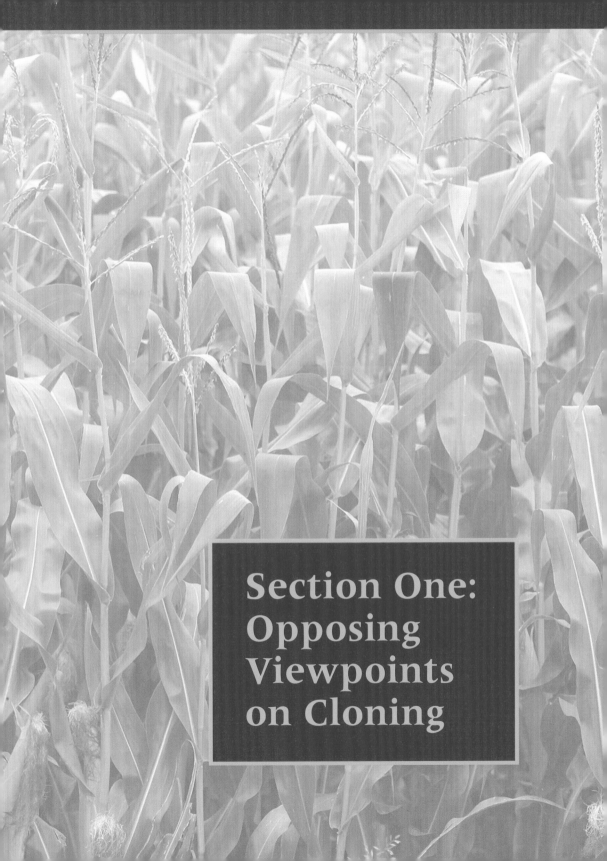

Section One:
Opposing
Viewpoints
on Cloning

Animal Cloning Has Many Potential Benefits

Linda Bren

Since the 1997 announcement that scientists had success-fully created a cloned sheep (named Dolly), researchers have created cloned cattle, pigs, goats, and other farm animals. In the following viewpoint Linda Bren explains the cloning process used to create animals and the reasons why farm-ers and scientists have pursued the technology. Through cloning it may be possible to select and reproduce the most desirable animals, reduce the number of unwanted animals, and possibly preserve and regenerate endangered species. Linda Bren is a writer for *FDA Consumer,* a publication of the Food and Drug Administration, a U.S. government agency that regulates the nation's food supply.

> ### Consider the following questions:
> 1. What are the different methods of cloning, according to Bren?
> 2. What is an epigenetic effect, according to the author?
> 3. How can cloning improve the welfare of ani-mals, according to Bren?

Full Flush is a celebrity. No one asks for his autograph, but they do ask for his progeny. Named for a winning poker hand, the aging grand champion bull can't meet the demand of all the cattle ranchers who want more like him. But the bull's clones may keep his legacy alive. Full Flush's five clones "were as normal and healthy as any

Linda Bren, "Cloning: Revolution or Evolution in Animal Production," *FDA Consumer,* vol. 37, May 2003.

calves I've ever raised," says rancher and veterinarian Donald Coover of Galesburg, Kan., who bottle-fed the young calves and raised them for the first six months of their lives. The calves, born in 2001, will soon be ready to propagate herds of high-quality beef cattle.

To the uninitiated, animal cloning may conjure up visions of strange, robot-like creatures, but real clones are far from this science-fiction fallacy. "This is just an assisted reproductive technology," says Mark Westhusin, Ph.D., director of the Reproductive Sciences Laboratory at Texas A&M University's College of Veterinary Medicine. "We're not trying to resurrect animals or get animals back."

"Clones are biological copies of normal animals," says Larisa Rudenko, Ph.D., a molecular biologist and risk assessor in the Food and Drug Administration's Center for Veterinary Medicine (CVM). "In theory, they're pretty close to identical twins of an adult animal." . . .

It's unlikely that you will eat a cloned animal anytime soon. At a cost of about $20,000 each to produce, clones are used for breeding—not for food. But some scientists and farmers are looking at the descendants of cloned cattle, pigs, goats and sheep as potential sources for food and clothing, if the FDA [Food and Drug Administration] gives the OK. . . .

The Cloning Process

Early methods of cloning in the 1970s involved a technology called embryo splitting, or blastomere separation. Embryos were split into several cells and then implanted into a surrogate mother for growth and development. But there were a limited number of splits that could be made, and only a few clones could be produced from one egg. The characteristics of the clone were also unpredictable because scientists were cloning from an embryo whose traits could not be predicted.

The practice of cloning took on new meaning in 1996 with the birth of Dolly the sheep, the world's first mammal cloned from an adult cell. Dolly was produced using

Ian Wilmut poses next to a museum display of his creation, Dolly the sheep, the first cloned mammal.

SCNT [somatic cell nuclear transfer] technology. Since the cloning of Dolly, this technology has been used to clone cattle, mice, goats, pigs, rabbits, and even a cat. Unlike the embryo splitting method, in theory, SCNT can be used to make an unlimited number of copies of one animal.

The SCNT process starts with an unfertilized egg, or oocyte. Scientists remove the oocyte's nucleus, which contains the egg's genes, or hereditary "instructions." What remains after removal of the nucleus is a cell that contains nutrients essential for embryo development and other cellular machinery waiting for a new set of instructions.

A somatic cell from the animal to be cloned—or in some cases, just the cell's nucleus—is cultured in an incubator and then injected under the coating of the unfertilized oocyte. (Somatic cells are any cells of the body except sperm and eggs.) Stimulated by a mild electrical pulse, the oocyte cytoplasm (everything in the cell but the nucleus) and the genetic material from the donated somatic cell combine. If fusion is successful, the resulting fused cell divides just as if it were a fertilized egg and produces an embryo. The embryo is placed in the uterus of a surrogate mother and, if development proceeds normally, an animal clone is born.

An embryonic sheep cell is inserted into a sheep egg as part of the cloning process.

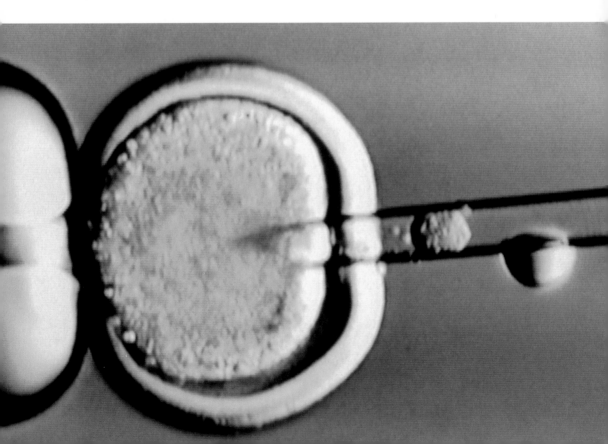

But there's a tricky part to this process, says Rudenko. The nucleus of the adult cell is specialized, or differentiated, for a particular function. "The nucleus has matured to a point where its instructions are 'locked away' in a configuration specific to the job that the cell is intended to perform," says Rudenko. "For example, a muscle cell has a different job from a liver cell, and it has a different set of instructions available to it. The complicated part of cloning that we don't fully understand is how those instructions get reset."

The unlocking and resetting of instructions without making changes to the genetic code is called epigenetic reprogramming. This process allows the cell to develop into a new organism instead of continuing to do its old specified cellular functions. And it's the epigenetic reprogramming that scientists haven't yet mastered and that accounts for frequent cloning failures.

Steven Stice, Ph.D., explains epigenetics as the propensity for different outcomes from identical DNA sequences. An example of an epigenetic effect in normal human birth is the different fingerprint patterns of identical twins, says Stice, a professor in the Animal and Dairy Science Department at the University of Georgia and chief scientific officer for ProLinia Inc., a livestock cloning company in Athens, Ga. Epigenetic changes are not unique to cloning but are more noticeable in clones, Stice adds. "Everything from in vitro fertilization to artificial insemination can have epigenetic effects."

Why Clone?

Proponents of livestock cloning see it benefiting consumers, producers, animals and the environment.

"The consumer is looking for a nutritious and wholesome product provided to them in a repeatable and reliable manner and produced in a humane and ethical way," says Coover, who also owns and manages SEK Genetics Inc., a beef cattle semen distribution company. "If a con-

sumer spends $30 on a steak dinner at a restaurant, they expect a great steak, but don't always get it."

For farmers whose livelihoods depend on selling high-quality meat and dairy products, cloning can offer a tremendous advantage, says Coover. It gives them the ability to preserve and extend proven, superior genetics. They can select and propagate the best animals—beef cattle that are fast-growing, have lean but tender meat, and are disease-resistant; dairy cows and goats that give lots of milk; and sheep that produce high-quality wool. Through cloning, it would be possible to predict the characteristics

Advocates believe cloning would provide farmers with the best farm animals and offer improved products to consumers. Pictured here is a litter of cloned piglets.

of each animal, rather than taking the chance that sexual reproduction and its gene reshuffling provide.

Coover compares the process of identifying a superior animal to spinning a giant roulette wheel. "Sometimes you win, sometimes you lose, and sometimes you hit the jackpot." But a producer cannot tell if he's hit the jackpot with a young animal. "It's like trying to identify the school kid in the second grade who is going to grow up to solve the riddle of cancer," says Coover. "A rancher may think he has a good bull, but that bull has to sire calves, the calves have to mature and produce calves of their own, and this has to occur for several generations to know that it's not a fluke. By that time, the bull is dead and gone, and its genetics are lost to the industry." Through SCNT cloning, even deceased animals can be cloned if a tissue sample is preserved in life or within a short time after death.

Cloning has the potential to improve the welfare of farm animals by eliminating pain and suffering from disease. "From time to time, in nature, you find a naturally disease-resistant animal," says Rudenko. "You can expand that genome through cloning, and then breed that resistance into the overall population and help eliminate major diseases in livestock."

Cloning can reduce the number of unwanted animals, such as veal calves, says Ray Page, chief scientific officer and biomedical engineer at Cyagra, a livestock cloning company. Veal calves are commonly surplus male offspring from dairy cows. Since the males don't produce milk, they are not as useful to the dairy industry and are turned into veal calves. Cloning can ensure the creation of more female offspring for dairy production.

An environmental benefit could result from cloning grass-fed instead of grain-fed animals. Grain-fed animals are

Cloning and Endangered Species

Advances in cloning offer a way to preserve and propagate endangered species that reproduce poorly in zoos until their habitats can be restored and they can be reintroduced to the wild.

Robert P. Lanza et al., *Scientific American*, November 19, 2000.

known to be better tasting and more tender, but once in a while, a high-quality grass-fed animal comes along. "If we can move our cattle-raising from a grain economy to a grass-fed economy, we can make food more efficiently and there are benefits to us as a society," says John Matheson, a toxicologist and environmentalist who serves as a senior regulatory review scientist for biotechnology in CVM. Grass is a soil-building crop. In addition to reducing erosion, grass does not need the quantities of fertilizers and pesticides required by grain. And because forage is cheaper than grain, production savings can be passed on to consumers.

— "Cloning can help spread the best genetics over larger populations of animals," says Stice. When farm animals are cloned, genetic diversity may be reduced, but cloning can also be a tool to preserve rare genetics in livestock and, potentially, wild animals. Stice encourages zoos and wildlife refuges to preserve the tissue of endangered species in the hopes that technology in the theoretical stage today can be developed to regenerate these species in the future.

Analyze the essay:

1. At what point does Bren provide an explanation of the cloning process? What did she accomplish in the preceding paragraphs?
2. How does the author organize her explanation of the cloning process? How effective do you think it is?

Animal Cloning Raises Serious Ethical Problems

Joseph Mendelson III

Joseph Mendelson III is legal director of the Center for Food Safety, a national nonprofit organization that works to support organic agriculture and lobbies against technologies it deems harmful to human health and the environment. The following viewpoint is excerpted from public commentary presented at an advisory committee of the Food and Drug Administration (FDA) on the risks of animal cloning. Mendelson argues that cloning animals for profit raises serious questions concerning animal welfare and food safety. Most cloning attempts have resulted in failure to attain live births—and those that survive suffer from many deformities and other health problems. He concludes his essay by calling for an immediate moratorium on the cloning of animals.

Consider the following questions:

1. What percentage of attempts at cloning animals succeed, according to Mendelson?
2. What is methylation, and what importance does it have to the cloning debate, according to the author?

The widespread commercialization of cloned animals poses numerous issues that need to be further addressed prior to the completion of any risk assessment and conclusions concerning commercialization. These issues include animal welfare issues, [and] in-depth edible product analysis. . . .

Joseph Mendelson III, "Initial Comments Concerning the Food and Drug Administration's Animal Cloning Risk Assessment," speech at the FDA Veterinary Medicine Advisory Committee, Rockville, MD, November 4, 2003. Copyright © 2003 by Joseph Mendelson III. Reproduced by permission.

Issues of Animal Welfare

The cloning of animals represents a fundamental change in our relationship with animals. The relationship changes human interaction with animals from an assistant in reproduction to a wholesale creator of genetic "replicas" of existing animals. The results of this relational change manifest themselves in the abhorrent animal suffering, a cruelty that will grow should cloning become a widespread commercial venture.

Ian Wilmut and his team of scientists implanted 277 cloned sheep embryos in surrogate ewes, from which only thirteen pregnancies resulted and Dolly was the only

A researcher implants a sheep embryo into a carrier ewe.

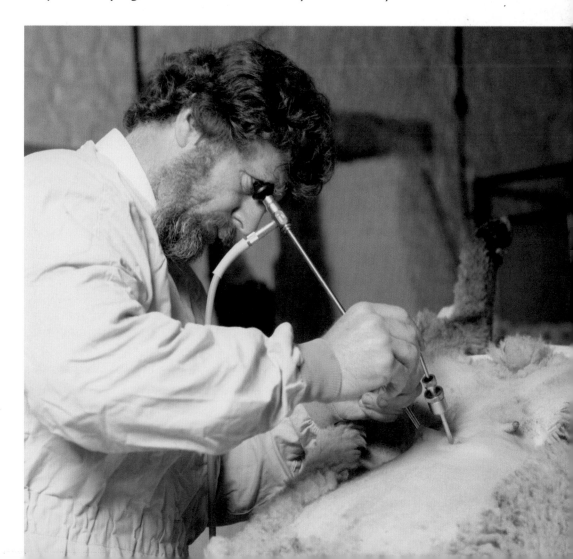

successful birth. Even after several years of additional research and the development of new methods for extracting and transferring genetic material, well over 99% of all cloning attempts still fail. Even when nuclear transfers produce embryos that are successfully implanted in surrogates, only 3% to 5% of these pregnancies produce offspring that live to adulthood. . . .

Cloned livestock that manage to survive birth tend to require more care than those sexually reproduced. Cloned calves, piglets, and lambs often require neonatal glucose infusions to treat hypoglycemia or oxygen treatments to offset hypoxia. Jonathan Hill, who has worked on cattle cloning at Cornell University, suspects that 25% to 50% of clones are born having been deprived of normal levels of oxygen. The neonatal condition of most clones is so poor, Rebecca Krisher, an animal reproduction specialist at Purdue University, says, "Almost all of these animals, if born on a farm without a vet hospital, . . . probably wouldn't survive."

The tremendous suffering of animal clones also impacts their surrogate hosts. Most cloned livestock also exhibit a condition known as "large-offspring syndrome," which results in overly stressful deliveries for the surrogate mothers. Because of their large size, a higher than normal percentage of clones are delivered via cesarean section. In one documented cattle cloning project, three out of 12 surrogate mothers died during pregnancy.

Even the cloned animals that survive to be born are likely to suffer a wide range of health problems. One example is a sheep cloned by Ian Wilmut and his team, the same group who brought Dolly into the world. This much less heralded sheep, born not long after Dolly, had a malformed respiratory tract and was soon euthanized. In fact, such abnormalities are common. Late in 2002, scientists at the New Zealand government's AgResearch reported that 24% of the cloned calves born at the facility died between birth and weaning. This compares to a 5% mortality rate for non-cloned calves. Another 5% of cloned calves died after weaning, compared to 3% of sexually reproduced calves.

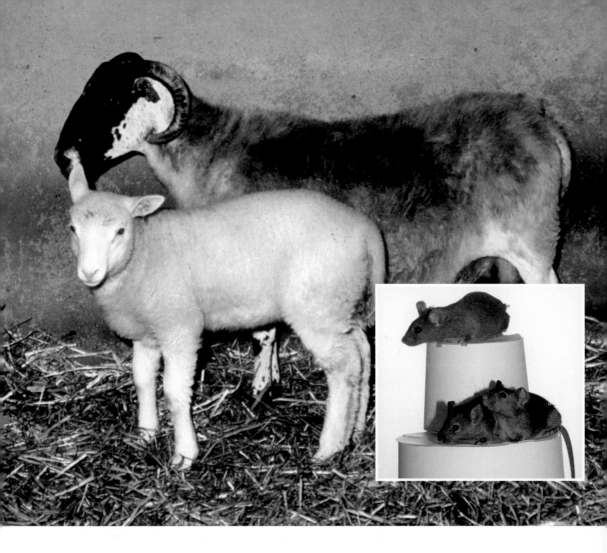

One review of scientific literature, authored by executives at the commercial cloning lab Advanced Cell Technology, found that nearly 25% of cow, sheep, swine, and mouse clones showed severe developmental problems soon after birth. However, the vast majority of the studies considered for this review had follow-up periods of only a few weeks or months. Many later-developing health problems would not be reflected.

These results clearly indicate that cloning has a significant and overwhelming impact on the animals involved in the process. Consumers and the public have consistently rejected the animal suffering caused by cloning based upon moral grounds. . . .

Dolly the sheep, pictured here with her surrogate mother, had to be euthanized due to disease. Many other cloned mammals, including these mice, have suffered from developmental problems.

Issues of Food Safety

In addition to the animal welfare issues, data concerning the health of adult clone animals raises the specter of significant unresolved issues of food safety. Recent research shows that even clones seeming healthy at birth may not be as normal as they appear. Scientists at Tokyo's National Institute of Infectious Diseases found that cloned mice had significantly shorter life spans than normal mice. The research team raised 12 apparently healthy cloned mice and seven

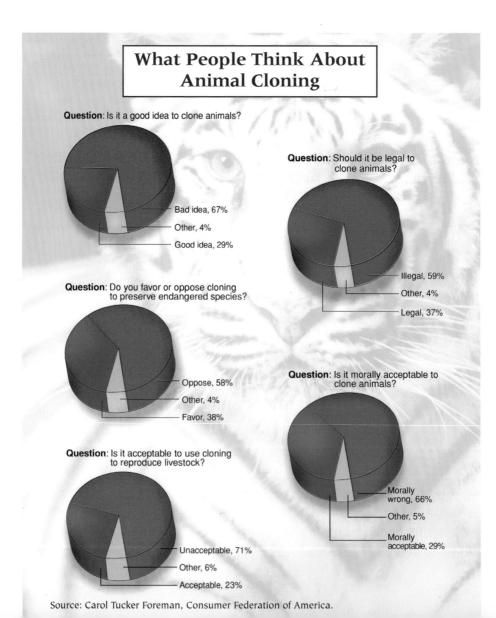

What People Think About Animal Cloning

Question: Is it a good idea to clone animals?

Bad idea, 67%
Other, 4%
Good idea, 29%

Question: Should it be legal to clone animals?

Illegal, 59%
Other, 4%
Legal, 37%

Question: Do you favor or oppose cloning to preserve endangered species?

Oppose, 58%
Other, 4%
Favor, 38%

Question: Is it morally acceptable to clone animals?

Morally wrong, 66%
Other, 5%
Morally acceptable, 29%

Question: Is it acceptable to use cloning to reproduce livestock?

Unacceptable, 71%
Other, 6%
Acceptable, 23%

Source: Carol Tucker Foreman, Consumer Federation of America.

sexually reproduced mice in a controlled laboratory environment. At about 300 days after birth, the first cloned mouse died. Within 800 days of birth, 10 of the 12 clones had died, while six of the seven sexually reproduced mice were still thriving. Autopsies revealed that the clones died from a variety of maladies, including liver failure, pneumonia due to weak immune systems, and cancer.

Late-developing health problems are not confined to mouse clones. In fact, Dolly, often touted as livestock cloning's greatest success story, developed premature arthritis. Even more seriously, in February this year [2003] veterinarians at the Roslin Institute decided to euthanize Dolly after diagnosing her with a progressive lung disease. Dolly was only six years old. Researchers said that her normal life expectancy would have been 11 or 12 years.

The most likely causes of clones' prenatal and postnatal defects are genetic abnormalities that arise during fetal development. Rudolf Jaenisch and colleagues at Massachusetts Institute of Technology's Whitehead Institute determined that cloned mice in their study had hundreds of improperly expressed genes. These resulted in a wide variety of abnormalities, ranging from the very subtle to the catastrophic. With so-called "imprinted genes," those that in a normal offspring only one copy—either from the mother or the father—is "switched on," Jaenisch found that nearly half "were incorrectly expressed." Though his experiments dealt only with cloned mice, Jaenisch concluded that genetic abnormalities were most likely responsible for the dismal success rates of cattle, sheep, and swine cloning efforts. "There is no reason in the world to assume that any other mammal . . . would be different from mice," he said. . . .

Methylation

In normally reproduced animals, a methylation switches certain genes off as the animal matures and the functions encoded by those genes are no longer necessary. Methylation also plays a role in the proper expression of imprinted genes. Because SCNT [somatic cell nuclear transfer] cloning uses genetic material from mature cells, the methylation pattern in these clones is often quite different than in animals that develop as normal embryos. While scientists try to "reprogram" the adult genetic material to act as if it were embryonic DNA, a group of South Korean scientists who studied SCNT cloned cow embryos detected no indications of methylation; they found this resulted in unusual patterns of genetic imprinting. The research team concluded that this incomplete genetic reprogramming could be one reason for the high failure rate of animal cloning.

Cloning May Not Save Endangered Species

If a species were truly to be rescued through cloning, some animals would need to be re-established in the wild. But, to introduce an animal back into a stressed ecosystem is questionable under the best of circumstances, and may even be an act of cruelty.

Britt Bailey, "Cloning the Gaur," Center for Ethics and Toxics, 2000, www.cetos.org.

A second study, presented in the June 2001 issue of *Genesis*, also showed abnormal methylation in clones, leading to unpredictable health problems, including overgrown placentas, increased body weight, and respiratory, blood or immune system problems. "No matter what you do, cloning changes these methylation flags," said one scientist. Jaenisch and his colleagues at the Whitehead Institute concluded that improper methylation caused the abnormalities they found with imprinted genes in their cloned mice. "Even apparently normal clones have an abnormal regulation of many genes," Jaenisch said. "Completely normal clones may be the exception." In fact, improper methylation may be cloning's fatal flaw. Writing in *Science,* Wilmut and Jaenisch state that there is no way now or for the foreseeable future for scientists to detect whether these reprogramming errors have occurred. . . .

Many scientists are concerned that these subtle and not-so-subtle "imprinting errors" raise as yet unresolved safety issues concerning the food products from cloned livestock. Ian Wilmut has said that commercial production of meat and dairy products from cloned animals should not begin until large-scale, controlled trials have been conducted. Cloners now working on dairy production say they are comparing the milk from their clones with natural milk, but Wilmut told the magazine *New Scientist* that study of cloned animals should look not only at milk, but also at the animals' health profiles and life spans. Wilmut warned that even small imbalances in an animal's hormone, protein, and fat levels could compromise the quality and safety of meat and milk. . . .

Call for a Cloning Moratorium

For consumers, commercial livestock cloning could inundate the food supply with novel products that have not been safety tested and have raised safety concerns among some of the leading scientists in the cloning field. For farm animals, the spread of cloning is likely to bring genetic defects, premature aging, and widespread suffering. Meanwhile, . . . regulators seem poised to place the interests of a few biotech firms over those of small farmers, consumers, and farm animals.

As a result of the inadequacies described above, the FDA should immediately institute a moratorium on the commercialization and marketing of milk and other edible products derived from cloned animals or their progeny.

Analyze the essay:

1. Mendelson starts his essay by listing examples of pre- and postnatal health problems of cloned animals, questioning the origin of these problems. What does he do in the second half of his essay?
2. Mendelson is addressing his comments to the U.S. government agency charged with regulating food safety. How does he link the issues of animal welfare and food safety? Is he convincing in joining these issues?

Cloning Humans Can Be Ethical

George Dvorsky

In late 2002 a somewhat obscure religious sect called the Raelians announced the birth of Eve, a girl they presented as the first successfully cloned human being. The announcement was greeted with skepticism by some. The validity of their claim was never proven. The news, however, did result in discussion about the ethics of human cloning. In the following viewpoint, philosopher and writer George Dvorsky predicts that the unorthodox background of the Raelians and the actions of other maverick scientists pursuing reproductive human cloning may result in a public backlash against the entire goal of cloning. Such a reaction would be unfortunate, he argues, because human cloning could, if developed responsibly, be a good thing for infertile and gay couples desiring genetic children of their own. Dvorsky is the deputy editor of Betterhumans.com, an editorial production company that provides information and analysis on scientific and technological trends and their impact on humanity's future.

Consider the following questions:

1. How did most people react to the announcement of Eve's birth, according to Dvorsky?
2. How did the Raelian religion become involved with cloning, according to the author?
3. What are some of the potential benefits of human reproductive cloning, according to Dvorsky?

Well it finally happened. The day I had been both eagerly anticipating and dreading arrived at long last: On December 27, 2002, the Raelian religious sect

Cloning pioneer Ian Wilmut has argued that attempts to clone humans are premature.

announced the arrival of a baby girl, Eve, who was the first successfully cloned human being in history. . . .

As . . . someone who promotes personal reproductive freedoms, I had been quietly anticipating the birth of the first human clone. It's probably safe to say that I'm in a minority; upon news of Eve's birth, most people offered blanket condemnations simply due to the fact that she's a clone, which somehow to them makes her less than human.

Once all the irrational brouhaha dies down over cloning, people will come to see it as just another beneficial reproductive option not unlike in vitro fertilization.

But unfortunately, the Raelians and their biotech company Clonaid have cloned humans about 10 years too early. The science of cloning is still in its infancy, and virtually every animal that has been cloned to date has had some sort of defect or abnormality.

In these early and premature days of human cloning, the pending public backlash will surely fall upon all groups who promote biotechnological advances. . . . We must act appropriately.

The Science of Human Cloning

Human cloning involves taking a woman's egg and removing its nucleus, which contains most of her DNA. The resulting hollow egg can be repopulated with the nucleus from another human's cell. Electrical stimulation or chemicals then cause the cells to fuse and grow.

No one quite understands how or why, but the process also switches the transferred nucleus cell back to an earlier state. The resulting embryo grows in a dish for a few days and can then be implanted into a woman's womb, where it will grow into a complete human baby.

There's no mystical voodoo involved, no hocus-pocus. There's no transmigration of the human soul. We can look at human clones as delayed twins. Yes, twins are identical genetic copies of each other. And yet, somehow, miraculously, life goes on in their presence.

Underdeveloped and Unethical

As of this writing, however, virtually every cloned animal has been born with some sort of defect or abnormality. That's if they make it to birth in the first place. The majority die in the womb.

Cloning pioneer Ian Wilmut of the Roslin Institute has carefully recorded such problems in lambs. Even after seemingly healthy lambs are born, they soon exhibit problems. For example, some can't stop panting, as if they have just run across a field.

In cloned animals of all different species there have been a variety of abnormalities, including problems with the kidneys, liver, heart, blood vessels, skin, musculature of the body wall and immune system. There are also problems with gigantism and many limb and facial abnormalities. . . .

For Roslin Institute Science Director Harry Griffin, such a fate should be a reality check for anyone who wants to clone a human.

Yet, unfortunately, not everyone is interested in reality.

In 1995 Morag became one of the first sheep cloned using embryonic cells. She died in 2000, and she was mounted for a display in a museum in Scotland.

Meet the Raelians and Maverick Scientists

On December 13, 1973, while commuting to his job as a sportswriter, Claude Vorilhon, who now goes by the moniker Rael, decided to drive past his office and stop at a nearby volcano in Auvergne, France.

According to Rael, once at the volcano he saw the flashing white light of a conical spaceship which opened its hatch to reveal a green alien with longish dark hair. Rael climbed aboard the spaceship where he was entertained by voluptuous female robots and learned that the first human beings were created by aliens called Elohim, who also cloned themselves.

And here comes the good part: the super-being Elohim, will return in 2025 to Jerusalem and liberate from earthly sorrows people with the "proper" awareness. The aliens, speaking in fluent French of course, instructed Rael to begin his religious movement. "Cloning is the key to eternal life," claims Rael.

Claude Vorilhon, aka Rael, founded Clonaid in 1997 to pursue human cloning.

The Raelian cult now claims 55,000 devotees world-wide and operates its own theme park, UFOland, near Montreal. During the 1990s, the province of Quebec granted religious status to the group. In addition to their emphasis on cloning, the Raelians advocate an extremely laissez-faire attitude towards sex. It was the aliens, after all, who informed Rael that "sensual meditation" was "the key to mastering the harmonizing possibilities in the brain, given to us by those who designed the human." A good form for such meditation would be sexual, he was told.

Yup, let's not mince words: these guys are wacky.

And soon after the announcement of Dolly in 1997, they established the first human cloning company, Clonaid. . . .

Cultish fanatics and their misguided biologists aside, there are a number of vainglorious scientists who seem to be involved in a race for the history books.

Italian doctor Severino Antinori and his American partner Panos Zavos discuss the possibility of human cloning at a 2001 panel discussion in Washington, D.C.

Scientists such as the Italian fertility doctor Severino Antinori and his American partner Panos Zavos appear to foam at the mouth over the prospect of being the first to clone a human being. . . .

Human Cloning Will Be a Good Thing

Yet, while we're condemning current cloning attempts, we must be careful not to condemn human cloning itself.

Human cloning will someday be a good thing. For infertile couples who cannot make babies with sperm and eggs, human cloning is a medical breakthrough that could provide them children of their own. Similarly, it will help gay couples produce biological offspring. It will also help in cases where a parent has an inheritable genetic defect and reproductive cloning would provide a better chance of having a healthy child.

Humans deserve the right to clone themselves should they choose, so long as the process isn't harmful. I can't see parents of clones being any less loving and caring than parents of regular children.

So long as reproductive cloning is left in the hands of responsible scientists, and the experiments are conducted with the utmost of safety in mind, the prospect of human cloning and all its benefits may someday become reality.

Analyze the essay:

1. Dvorsky attempts to distance his own position from that of the Raelians and others promoting human cloning. How does he condemn current cloning attempts but not human cloning itself?
2. Does Dvorsky satisfactorily explain, in your opinion, the difference between "responsible" and "irresponsible" cloning research?

Human Cloning Should Be Discouraged

Christian Century

In January 2001 Italian fertility specialist Severino Antinori and U.S. scientist Panayiotis Zavos announced their plans to be the first scientists to clone a human being. The following viewpoint is taken from an editorial in the *Christian Century* reacting to that news and to the notion that humans should have the right to clone. The authors endorse Roman Catholic Church pronouncements on the immorality and danger of human reproductive cloning. They conclude that human reproductive cloning is a clear threat to human dignity. *Christian Century* is a Protestant publication.

Consider the following questions:

1. What argument for cloning may people find difficult to resist, according to the authors?
2. What reasons do the authors give to support their contention that cloning undermines human dignity?

Margaret Talbot, writing recently in the *New York Times*, reports that many scientists expect a cloned human to be introduced within five years. "It's relatively easy to set up a lab and find someone competent to carry out the procedure," one researcher told Talbot. "From a technical point of view," said another, "cloning a human being would be a very simple thing."

Experiments on human cloning are probably taking place somewhere right now. Though U.S. law precludes federal

Demonstrators in Germany protest the government's decision to grant cloning scientists 100,000 euros in funding. The sign reads, "100,000 euros for the destruction of life."

money from being spent on such research, and [some] states have outlawed cloning for reproductive purposes, the field remains wide open to privately funded efforts.

Talbot notes that she has encountered enormous longing for human cloning, especially among parents who have lost a young child. A casual search of the Internet turns up fervent endorsements of cloning, for utilitarian and sentimental reasons. Above all, one encounters an attitude of Why not? As one writer for the online magazine *Slate* wrote, "If humans have the right to reproduce, what right does society have to limit the means?" Given the contemporary commitment to individual rights and choices, this argument will be difficult to resist.

A Threat to Human Dignity

Nevertheless, human cloning is a profound threat to human dignity. The practice will inevitably result in a confusion of basic human roles and in the objectification of persons. Cloning is one of the clearest examples possible of treating an individual as a means.

Proponents of cloning occasionally point out that cloned humans are already among us in the form of

Senator Sam Brownback, a sponsor of legislation banning all forms of human cloning, looks over a stack of anti-cloning petitions.

twins—people with identical sets of DNA—so what's the problem? Besides avoiding the fact that natural twins are always siblings, whereas a clone could be the twin of a parent or grandparent, this observation ignores a crucial moral difference: natural twins arrive as rare creations, not as specifically designed products.

The most decisive Christian response to human cloning has come from the Vatican. It has said that cloning . . . will foster the idea that "some individuals can have total dominion over the existence of others, to the point of programming their biological identity." And as the practice of cloning spreads, the Vatican warns, the conviction will grow that "the value of man and woman does not depend on their personal identity but only on those biological qualities that can be appraised and therefore selected."

Some of this language may be unfamiliar to Protestants, who historically have resisted Roman Catholic natural-law reasoning on matters of reproduction. However, the Vatican has identified the range of issues at stake and offered a powerful challenge to Protestant ethicists to offer their own arguments. It has also provided a strong rebuttal to any who would say simply, Why not?

Analyze the essay:
1. How do the authors respond to the contention that clones are simply a form of twins?
2. Does citing Vatican teachings on cloning strengthen or weaken the authors' arguments, in your view? Why or why not?

Reproductive and Therapeutic Cloning Are Fundamentally Different

Gregory E. Kaebnick

Efforts by the U.S. Congress to ban human cloning have failed to pass in part because of disagreements over what kinds of cloning should be banned. In the following viewpoint Gregory E. Kaebnick wants the public to distinguish between "reproductive cloning" and "therapeutic cloning." The first uses cloning technology to create an embryo that is transplanted to a uterus to grow into a new cloned individual. The public is generally opposed to this type of cloning. Therapeutic cloning (also called research cloning), on the other hand, creates an embryo that is then used as a source of scientific research and of embryonic stem cells. The author argues that a distinction should be made between the two types in order to avoid a total cloning ban that would set back scientific research on stem cell medical treatments. Kaebnick is a bioethics researcher and the editor of the Hastings Center Report, *a biomedical ethics journal.*

Consider the following questions:

1. How does the author explain the difference between therapeutic and reproductive cloning?
2. How have the public and scientific definitions of cloning diverged, according to Kaebnick?

Distinctions that require explanations tend to get lost in public debate, and the controversy over cloning is a perfect example.

Gregory E. Kaebnick, "Let's Define Two Kinds of Cloning," *Seattle Post-Intelligencer,* January 3, 2003.

There are two fundamentally different types of cloning—"reproductive cloning" and "therapeutic cloning"—but the distinction between them is in danger of getting lost. And if it does, it could be a severe blow to science.

The media and scientists have been careful in every report to explain that reproductive cloning refers to the creation of an embryo using a technique known as somatic cell nuclear transfer. In this process, the nucleus of the cell from an adult is transferred into an egg whose own nucleus has been removed. The goal is to bring the embryo to term and produce a live baby.

The explainers of science have also been careful to spell out the ways in which therapeutic cloning differs

In this computer artwork, identical cloned human babies crawl out of an enormous test tube.

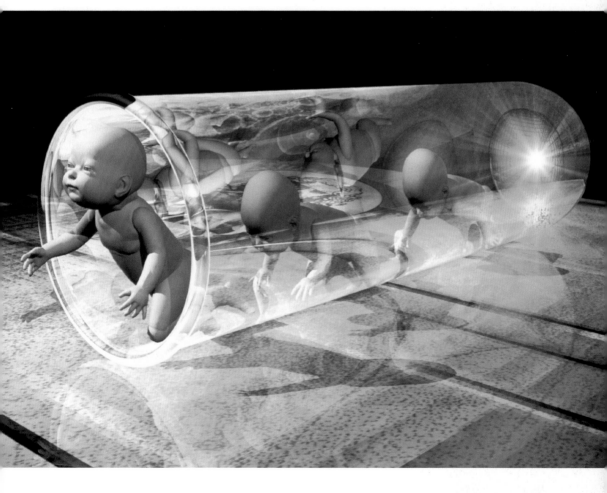

Supporters of therapeutic cloning wish to clone embryos in order to extract their stem cells (illustrated here).

from its counterpart. In this process, an embryo is created through the same technique, but with the goal of extracting stem cells from it and producing—someday, it is hoped—new medical therapies.

Of course, the fact that these explanations must be given over and over only shows how badly the distinction has failed to take root with the public.

Public vs. Scientific Definitions

As the controversy has heated up with the claim of the first human clone, the word cloning has come to mean, in the public's mind, the use of somatic cell nuclear transfer for artificial, asexual reproduction; to make a biologic copy of an existing organism.

Scientists themselves often use the word "cloning" casually to refer to any use of somatic cell nuclear transfer. But elsewhere in science, cloning refers to outcome rather than process: it denotes replication of some biologic entity—perhaps an organism, but perhaps only one cell, or perhaps just a stretch of DNA. This reproduction might involve somatic cell nuclear transfer or it might use some other technology.

The difficulty in making a distinction between reproductive and therapeutic cloning is showing up most evidently in two competing Senate bills. One . . . would ban all cloning research. The other . . . views cloning via its end result, and would allow therapeutic cloning while banning reproductive cloning.

Meanings of Words

Words are not always content with scientists' definitions of them. What percentage of Americans actually think of a tomato as a fruit rather than a vegetable? How often are bison called buffalo? In general, we can live with that sort of confusion—but when it comes to a politically charged issue like cloning, we can't.

So it might make sense for scientists to restrict their use of the word cloning to the reproductive type. This is exactly what Stanford University did when it denied that studies it planned to sponsor on somatic cell nuclear transfer would be cloning research. Scientists would only be creating stem cells, said university officials, not doing cloning. The claim was preposterous by scientific standard—that is, if cloning is defined by a laboratory technique.

What Medical Professionals Think About Cloning

Yes
No

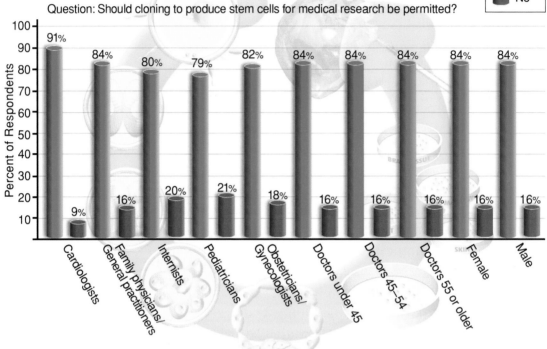

Question: Should cloning to produce stem cells for medical research be permitted?

Percent of Respondents

Cardiologists	91%	9%
Family physicians/General practitioners	84%	16%
Internists	80%	20%
Pediatricians	79%	21%
Obstetricians/Gynecologists	82%	18%
Doctors under 45	84%	16%
Doctors 45–54	84%	16%
Doctors 55 or older	84%	16%
Female	84%	16%
Male	84%	16%

Source: *Medical Economics*, October 11, 2002.

But if by "cloning" we mean a form of reproduction, it was exactly right. Of course, only scientists themselves can decide how they will use their terms of art. A more vexing problem is what the rest of us should do.

A Tinge of Apprehension

Even if the public understands the scientific differences between types of cloning, I have my doubts that it will be enough. People are still likely to see therapeutic cloning as derivative from reproductive cloning: it starts the same way, although the process is interrupted and the new organism is put to other uses.

Thus we will view therapeutic cloning with a tinge of the apprehension that reproductive cloning arouses in us, and a total ban on cloning correspondingly will grow more attractive. Perhaps in the end scientists should let the public use the word cloning in the sense it wants to and focus instead on making the distinction between cloning and stem cell research.

Both processes can, at certain stages, employ the same laboratory techniques, but then they follow different paths and have different outcomes. And in this case, it is outcomes, not laboratory techniques, that matter.

Analyze the essay:

1. Kaebnick contends that the differences between the two types of cloning are "fundamental." How does he explain the distinction?

2. Kaebnick suggests that scientists avoid the word *cloning* when discussing stem cell research. After reading his explanation, do you believe such a policy is justified?

Reproductive and Therapeutic Cloning Are Fundamentally the Same

Donal P. O'Mathuna

Donal P. O'Mathuna is a professor of chemistry and bioethics at Mount Carmel College of Nursing in Columbus, Ohio. In the following viewpoint, he criticizes those who make a distinction between therapeutic cloning and reproductive cloning—and the idea that the former can be permitted. In both cases, he argues, the same procedure is used to create human embryos. The only difference is that in therapeutic or research cloning, the cloned embryo is not implanted in a women's womb and brought to term but is instead destroyed for its cells. All forms of human cloning are dehumanizing and should be banned, O'Mathuna concludes.

> ### Consider the following questions:
> 1. What have researchers from Advanced Cell Technology announced regarding human cloning, according to O'Mathuna?
> 2. At what point is the cloning procedure over, according to the author?
> 3. What ethic does cloning promote, according to O'Mathuna?

After Dolly the sheep was cloned, many people voiced concern about attempting the procedure with humans. But that hasn't stopped some scientists. Researchers at

Advanced Cell Technology in Massachusetts have announced [in November 2001] the cloning of human embryos.

They urged us not to worry, though, claiming this is not human cloning. They "only" cloned embryos. Long before these come to term, they will be destroyed as part of the push to develop therapies from stem-cell research.

They call this procedure therapeutic cloning, to distinguish it from reproductive cloning, which would produce cloned babies. The moral problems with cloning, these researchers claim, do not apply to therapeutic cloning.

These terms represent an attempt to manipulate language to get around the almost universal abhorrence of human cloning. Explaining the procedures involved will show that therapeutic cloning is, first and foremost, cloning. Its use on humans is, therefore, human cloning.

The Cloning Procedure

The procedure used to produce Dolly, and with these human cells, is called somatic cell nuclear transfer, or

In 2001 a demonstrator dressed as the Grim Reaper protests outside the offices of Advanced Cell Technology after the company announced that it had cloned human embryos.

SCNT. Let's say Johnny and Mary want to produce a clone. Mary's eggs and Johnny's sperm contain only half of their genetic material, but all their other cells contain a complete copy of their genes. These cells are called somatic cells, and they store their genetic material in each cell's nucleus. In SCNT, researchers would remove the nucleus from some of Mary's eggs and replace it with a nucleus from Johnny's somatic cells. The resulting cells are zapped with electricity, and the hope is that some of them will grow and develop just like any other fertilized egg. These embryos, though, would have exactly the same genetic make-up as Johnny; they would be clones of Johnny.

At this point, the cloning procedure is over. A cloned embryo will either grow and develop and come to term,

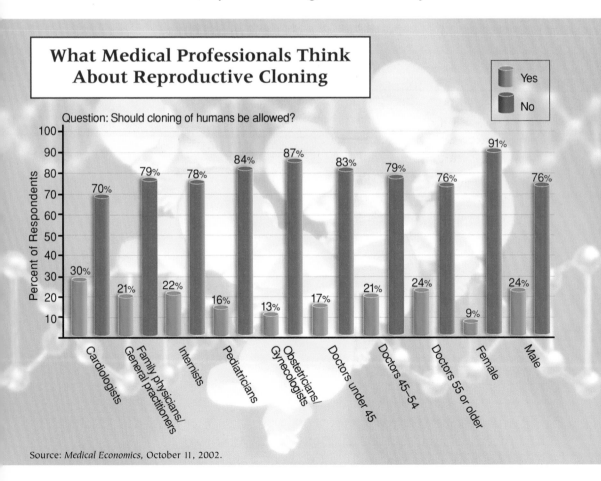

What Medical Professionals Think About Reproductive Cloning

Yes

No

Question: Should cloning of humans be allowed?

Percent of Respondents

Cardiologists: 30%, 70%
Family physicians/General practitioners: 21%, 79%
Internists: 22%, 78%
Pediatricians: 16%, 84%
Obstetricians/Gynecologists: 13%, 87%
Doctors under 45: 17%, 83%
Doctors 45–54: 21%, 79%
Doctors 55 or older: 24%, 76%
Female: 9%, 91%
Male: 24%, 76%

Source: *Medical Economics*, October 11, 2002.

Gamble. © 2005 by Ed Gamble. Reproduced by permission.

or will die from natural or humanly inflicted causes. Whether Johnny and Mary are justified in killing their clone or allowing him to come to term is a second ethical question they must address. Whatever their answer, it does not justify their cloning Johnny in the first place.

Therapeutic cloning, then, is a disingenuous term, designed to distract people from the fact that SCNT applied to human cells, for whatever reason, is human cloning. Leon Kass, head of the presidential commission on stem-cell research, has written that this term is used to "obscure the fact that the clone will be 'treated' only to exploitation and destruction, and that any potential future beneficiaries and any future 'therapies' are at this point purely hypothetical."

Researchers claim they need therapeutic cloning to realize the benefits of stem-cell research. If Johnny had a disease that stem cells might someday cure, his body could reject another person's stem cells, just as transplanted organs can be rejected. To avoid this, Johnny's clone would be sacrificed to produce stem cells that are

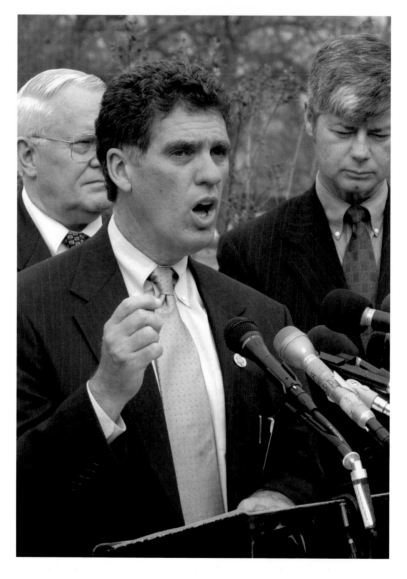

Congressmen Dave Weldon (center), Bart Stupak (right), and Joe Pitts call for legislation to ban all forms of human cloning.

compatible with his body. Thus, the ethics of stem-cell research are intricately interwoven with human cloning.

But the hopes of therapeutic cloning far outdistance the reality. Ian Wilmut, the principal researcher involved with Dolly, declared that "attempts to clone human beings . . . are dangerous and irresponsible."

He should know. Although Dolly remains [as of 2001] healthy, another cloned sheep, born shortly after Dolly, was put down because of birth defects. She died without publicity, or a cute name. Animal cloning has an abysmally low success rate. Many clones are born with horrible deformities, and 95 percent to 99 percent of cloned embryos die before birth. Even mothers are at risk. Cows have died during pregnancy because the cloned calves grew excessively large within the womb. And no one knows whether abnormalities are transmitted to stem cells derived from cloned embryos.

We Should Ban All Cloning

The House of Representatives passed the Human Cloning Prohibition Act of 2001 to ban all cloning, whether therapeutic or reproductive. It hasn't become law because the Senate didn't take up the bill. Our society needs to ban human cloning to prevent the creation and destruction of human life, whether embryonic or more advanced.

Cloning dehumanizes humans, treating them like commodities to be manufactured and discarded as willed. This research promotes the utilitarian ethic that some members of the species can be used and destroyed if other members believe they have enough to gain. This ethic has caused untold pain and suffering throughout human history. We can prevent its progress by taking a strong stand against any form of human cloning.

Analyze the essay:

1. Why does O'Mathuna consider *therapeutic cloning* to be a "disingenuous term"? Do you agree or disagree with his explanation?
2. What arguments does the author make in the essay's closing sentences? Do these arguments directly follow the material in the preceding paragraphs, in your opinion? Explain.

Cloning and Stem Cell Research Can Save Human Lives

David Holcberg

Therapeutic cloning—cloning embryos to harvest their stem cells—is something that should be encouraged, argues David Holcberg in the following viewpoint. Embryonic stem cells are special cells that form at the very early stage of embryonic life. Holcberg argues that such stem cells may help cure diseases or even be induced to grow new skin, nerves, or organs. But such research, he explains, has been hindered by those who want to outlaw therapeutic cloning because it destroys potential humans. Holcberg maintains that the human embryos destroyed by cloning research are not actual human beings. A regard for the lives of actual people who may be helped or cured by stem cell research should outweigh any moral concerns about embryos, he concludes. Holcberg, a former civil engineer, is a writer for the Ayn Rand Institute in Irvine, California, an organization that promotes the philosophy of writer Ayn Rand.

Consider the following questions:

1. Who can benefit from therapeutic cloning, according to Holcberg?
2. What motivates opponents of human cloning research, according to the author?

On November 25 [2001] Advanced Cell Technology announced the creation of the first cloned human embryo. The company described its achievement as a crucial step in therapeutic cloning research, which aims at cloning new organs to replace damaged ones. Like healthy new skin for fire victims; or strong new bones for osteoporosis patients; or new retinas for blind people; or new spinal cords for paraplegics.

Amazingly, not everybody wants therapeutic cloning to succeed. Two hundred and sixty two members of the House of Representatives, for example, voted earlier this year [2001] to outlaw its practice. Our Congressmen set a punishment of up to ten years in jail for researchers and doctors who may dare clone a human cell in pursuit of medical cures.

What is their reason for banning therapeutic cloning? Aren't they aware of the life-saving potential of this technology?

Robert Lanza is the cofounder of Advanced Cell Technology, the company that first cloned human embryos.

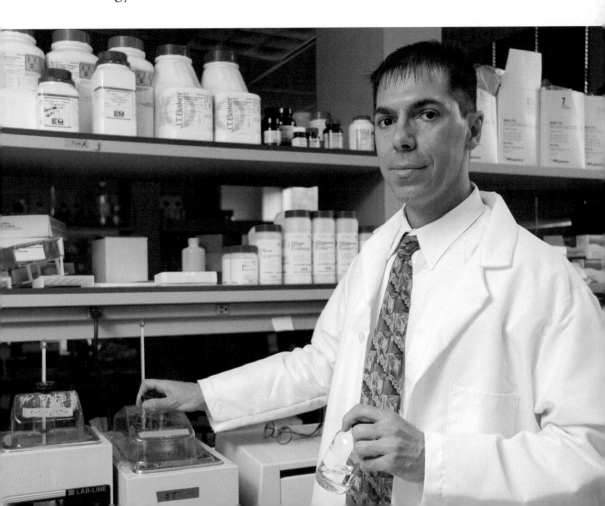

Oh, they are. The possible benefits of therapeutic cloning are undisputed even by its fiercest opponents. The reason most of them oppose therapeutic cloning is because it involves the manipulation and death of young human embryos, which they regard as akin to the manipulation and death of human beings.

But a human embryo is not a human being.

This can be literally seen just by looking at a human embryo, like the one that appeared in the December 2001 issue of *Scientific American*. If you get hold of a copy, you will see that the young embryo is smaller than the pin of a needle—just about the size of a grain of sand. You will also see that the embryo is not some sort of miniature human being, but merely a bundle of a dozen round cells

In this highly magnified image, a human embryo is shown at the ten-cell stage on the tip of a pin.

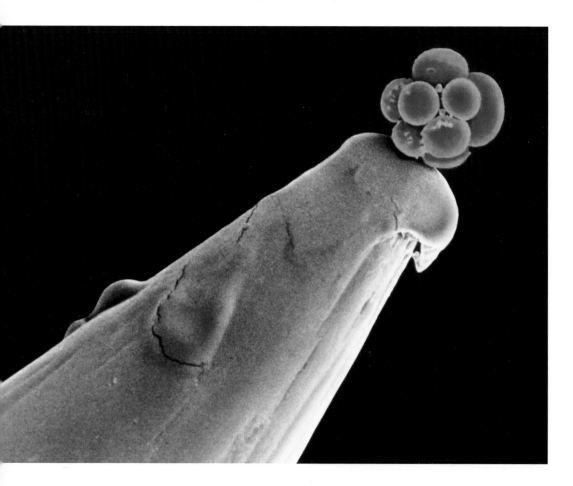

stuck together. The bundle has no legs, no arms, no torso, no neck and no head. It has no body. It has no human form. Once you see a young embryo as it is—a microscopic lump of cells—it becomes self-evident that it is not a human being at all.

The false premise that a human embryo is a human being comes up in the cloning debate in different guises, the most common being the assertion that "life begins at conception." Often spoken like a mantra, it appears to have a calming effect on the speaker, settling the issue in his mind. But if one would stop to think about it, one would realize that the life that begins at conception is not the life of a human being, but the life of an embryo. In retrospect you may say that your life began at your conception, but at that time there was no you.

> ## Stem Cell Cloning Should Not Be Outlawed
>
> **Because of its therapeutic potential, research that clones stem cells for medical purposes deserves our support. It should be publicly funded and better regulated, not outlawed.**
>
> Raymond Barglow, *Tikkun*, July/August 2002.

"Ok," some may concede, "the young embryo is not a human being. But it has the potential to become a human being. Shouldn't it then have the same right to life as a human being has?"

No. While it is true that a human embryo may have the potential to become a human being, as long as it is an embryo, it is not yet a human being. A human embryo is not a human being in the same way that a seed is not a tree, and that an egg is not a chicken. Things are what they are—not what they may come to be.

Not all opponents of therapeutic cloning, however, regard the status of the embryo as the central issue in this debate. Some oppose the technology because they fear it would eventually lead to cloning people. But even if they are right, it would be insane to ban therapeutic cloning, which may save countless lives, just because some people may decide to have babies that look like themselves.

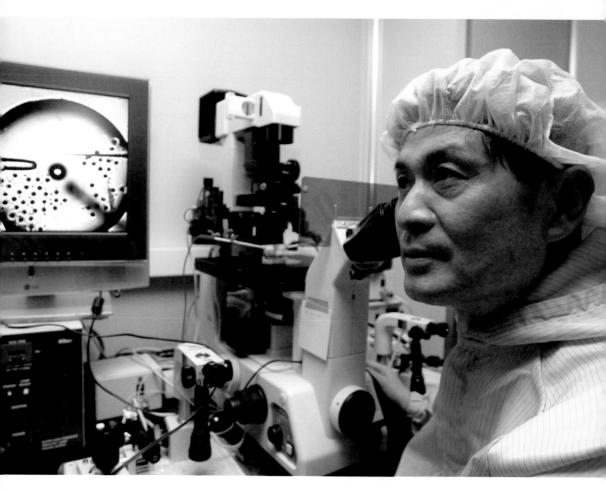

Hwang Woo-Suk is the leader of a team of Korean scientists that in 2004 cloned thirty human embryos. From one of the embryos they created a line of stem cells to be used for research.

In addressing the issue of cloning, President [George W.] Bush was absolutely right that "The moral issues posed by human cloning are profound and have implications for today and for future generations." The president was also right that "We must advance the promise and cause of science, but must do so in a way that honors and respects life."

Therapeutic Cloning Honors Life

Therapeutic cloning honors and respects life—human life. And any person who has true respect for human beings should think this issue through and stop advocating respect for human embryos.

Those who fall into the trap of equivocating between a human being and an embryo will end up sacrificing real human beings for microscopic clusters of cells. Embryos are not people, and treating them as if they were will end up costing human lives. One day, maybe not too far off in the future, you or someone you love may need a new heart or lung or liver to survive. If therapeutic cloning is banned, there will be no hope for you—or them.

Soon the Senate and the President will decide if the House of Representatives' ban on therapeutic cloning will stand. The choice they will face is clear: cloning and life, or prohibition and death. Let's make sure they pick the right one.

Analyze the essay:

1. What points does Holcberg make to support his belief that human embryos are not human beings?
2. At the article's conclusion, he equates cloning with life and its prohibition with death. How did he lead up to that conclusion? Do you agree or disagree? Why?

Cloning and Stem Cell Research Destroy Human Lives

Commonweal

The issues of cloning and stem cell research are interlinked because cloning can serve as a possible source of embryonic stem cells. The following viewpoint about stem cell research is excerpted from an editorial in *Commonweal*, a Catholic publication. The editors argue that some proponents of this line of research exaggerate its possible health benefits. They further contend that such research is morally objectionable because it destroys human life. The U.S. government should ban human cloning and other forms of stem cell research, the authors of this viewpoint conclude.

Consider the following questions:

1. How does the stem cell controversy echo earlier biomedical debates, according to the authors?
2. What general principles do the authors believe are violated by embryonic stem cell research?

"Ladies and Gentlemen: Today Only: The Elixir of Life! We have in these nearly invisible, no-bigger-than-the-period-at-the-end-of-this-sentence embryos the secret to long life and perfect health. These tiny cells—they call 'em blastocysts back in the lab—will cure the aches and pains, the ills of humankind. Neurologically degenerative conditions like Parkinson's and Alzheimer's, gone like smallpox! Autoimmune diseases like lupus and

In this illustration, a cloning researcher and two businessmen squeeze money from a strand of DNA.

rheumatoid arthritis, cured on diagnosis! The end of cancer! The end of diabetes as we know it! And, Ladies and Gentlemen, these cells, as miniscule as they appear today, will someday provide replacement parts for every nook and cranny of the human body, from hearts to hamstrings.

"You ask how anything so small could provide us with the gift of virtual immortality? Ladies and Gentlemen, give us your dollars and we will give you the answer."

Instructive, isn't it, how much scientists clamoring for federal funds sound like that quintessential American huckster, the snake-oil salesman?

We have heard this spiel before. In 1992, Congress held hearings on transplanting fetal brain cells, much like the hearings we saw in mid-July [2001] on embryonic stem cells. Suffering humanity, especially children, are exhibited to move the hearts of congressmen who wouldn't dare say "no" to Little Nell. Back in '92, proponents argued that fetal brain cells were the cure for Parkinson's and for most of the diseases and disabilities that today they say stem cells will remedy. In fact, transplanted fetal brain cells have turned out to be, well—snake oil. Congress

Ramirez. © 1998 by Copley News Service. Reproduced by permission.

approved, and fetal brain cells were duly injected into the brains of Parkinson's sufferers. The treatment did not work. More serious, it made the conditions of some 15 percent of patients far worse, and their standard medications less effective than they had been before the implantation.

This is not proof that fetal cells, stem cells, or cloned cells won't eventually do much that scientists have promised. But, as yet, there is meager evidence that they will. At the same time, tentative research results suggest that adult stem cells may offer respite from certain cancers, some injuries, and some chronic illnesses while avoiding the potential biological problems expected with embryo stem cells, namely tumors and transplant rejection. . . .

Nascent Human Life

That the . . . embryos are nascent human life, which must be destroyed in order to extract the stem cells, is, of course, a controversial matter, raising all the arguments and passions that surround the abortion issue. A human life has begun. But other profound questions are at stake; and the abortion cudgel tends to obscure them.

It is true these embryos are not human persons (which is why some pro-life senators and congressmen have come out in favor of federal funding for stem-cell research). But they are human life. . . . It is the fact of their humanness not their stage of development that should raise the most profound skepticism about the ultimate goal of embryo stem-cell research. Today we are promised cures from debilitating or fatal diseases; tomorrow replacement organs; and

President George W. Bush advocates banning both reproductive and therapeutic cloning.

the day after custom-designed progeny. By then we will be well on the road to the brave new world of control and standardization of human reproduction. This is a process of selection that can only destroy the fragile hold we humans have on a sense of our own dignity and singularity.

Proponents of stem-cell research argue that . . . we should use them for the benefit of the living who are suffering now. On the contrary, embryos should not be used in this way for the same reason that we would not cannibalize the heart, kidney, liver, or corneas of an unconscious person for transplantation purposes. In other words, as a matter of public policy, we would not sacrifice the life and/or dignity of one human, no matter its state of being or state of development, for the benefit of another.

If we do not draw a line now respecting human life in these embryos, the pressures on the president and Congress from researchers, investors, and the representatives of the ill and dying guarantee that no line will be drawn at all. Before adjourning, the House tried to draw one significant line by banning human cloning, but the Senate is unlikely to follow its lead. . . . In the meantime, the president should . . . work with Congress to appropriate a modest level of federal funding to support research on adult stem cells. This research has shown real potential and is being carried out now without raising the moral, legal, and biological problems of embryonic stem cells.

Analyze the essay:
1. What is the purpose of the opening paragraphs? Do you think their description of stem cell research supporters, such as David Holcberg (author of the previous viewpoint), is fair? Why or why not?
2. What future nightmare scenarios do the authors describe? Do you agree or disagree with their contention that these scenarios could happen? Explain.

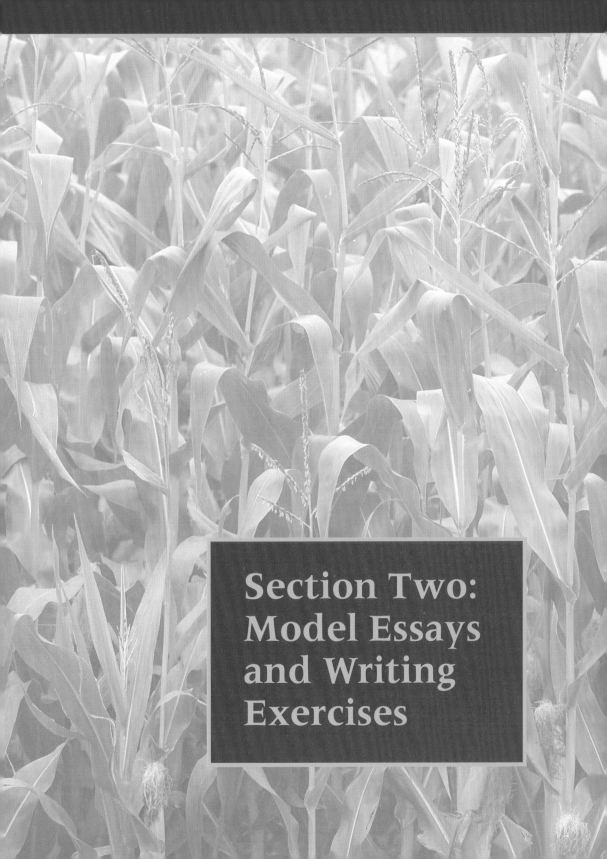

**Section Two:
Model Essays
and Writing
Exercises**

Expository Writing and the Five-Paragraph Essay

The previous section of this book provided samples of published persuasive writing on cloning. All were persuasive essays that made arguments or advocated a particular position about cloning. But all included elements of expository writing as well.

In the following section you will read some model expository essays on human cloning and do exercises that will help you write your own essay. To help you, this preface will identify the main components of five-paragraph essays (as well as longer pieces) and discuss how these components fit together. It also will briefly examine the differences and similarities between persuasive and expository writing and examine several distinct kinds of exposition.

Expository Essays vs. Persuasive Essays

Persuasive and expository essays share some similarities. Both can be about controversial topics. Both often involve research and the gathering of information and may include citations or quotations from various sources.

Where they differ is not so much on *structure* as in *purpose*. The purpose of expository writing is to impart factual information about a particular subject matter to the reader. The writer seeks to demonstrate his or her knowledge of a topic by communicating that knowledge to the reader. By contrast, the purpose of a piece of persuasive writing is to argue in favor of a particular viewpoint or position and to convince readers that your particular view is correct. The writer's intent is to persuade the reader to agree with the essay or even to take a course of action. In the real world, one often finds the two modes of writing intermixed. Sometimes the trickiest part of researching and writing about controversial topics such as cloning is discerning where exposition ends and persuasion begins.

Types of Expository Writing

Writing educators have identified several different types of expository writing that can be analyzed at both the sentence and paragraph level. Some of these structure types include definition, process/how-to, illustration, classification, and problem/solution. Examples of these types of expository writing can be found in the viewpoints in the preceding section.

Definition refers to simply telling what something is. Definitions can be encompassed in a sentence or a paragraph. Linda Bren quotes a scientist defining animal clones as "biological copies of normal animals," while George Dvorsky refers to human clones as "delayed twins." At other times, definitions may take a paragraph or more. Some definitions—especially those of abstract concepts—can serve as the topics of entire essays. Viewpoint Five, for example, is dedicated to the definition of cloning.

A *classification* essay or paragraph describes and clarifies relationships between things by placing them in different categories based on their similarities and differences. This can be a good way of organizing and presenting information. An example of classification can be found in Viewpoint One by Linda Bren and her description of the benefits of livestock cloning. Bren creates categories of benefits to consumers, producers, animals, and the environment. She provides a paragraph or two explaining in some detail how cloning can help in each area. Joseph Mendelson III takes a similar classification approach in providing an opposite view, classifying the problems of farm animal cloning into two categories: issues of animal welfare and questions of food safety. Sometimes classification becomes part of the general dispute. Viewpoints Five and Six provide an example in which the authors disagree on whether to divide cloning into "reproductive" and "research" categories.

A *process* essay or paragraph looks at how something is done. The writer presents events or steps in a chronological or ordered sequence of steps. Process writing can either inform the reader of a past event or a process by which something was made or instruct the reader on how to do something. Bren uses six paragraphs in the middle of Viewpoint One to explain the somatic cell nuclear transfer (SCNT) process of cloning. Dvorsky, in Viewpoint Three, devotes two paragraphs to the same process, referring to how human cloning might work.

Illustration is one of the simplest and most common patterns of expository writing. Simply put, it explains by giving specific and concrete examples. It is an effective technique for making one's writing both more interesting and more intelligible. For example, in Viewpoint Seven David Holcberg not only writes in general that stem cells can help humans, but he also gives specific examples: a blind person may receive a new eye, a burn victim new skin, a paraplegic new nerve cells.

Problem/solution refers to when the author raises a problem or a question, then uses the rest of the paragraph or essay to answer the question or provide possible solutions to the problem. It can be an effective way of drawing in the reader while imparting information.

The Components of the Five-Paragraph Essay

Whether persuasive or expository, five-paragraph essays— a favored essay structure commonly used in school assignments and tests—generally have the same structure. Every five-paragraph essay begins with an introduction, ends with a conclusion, and features three supporting paragraphs in the middle.

The introduction presents the essay's topic and thesis statement. The topic is the issue or subject discussed in the essay. All the essays in this book are about the same topic—cloning. The thesis, or thesis statement, is the central argument or point that the essay is trying to make about the topic. The essays are organized in support of this idea. The essays in this book all have different thesis statements because they are making differing arguments about cloning.

The thesis statement should be a clear statement that tells the reader what the essay will be about. For persuasive articles, the thesis is the particular argument or assertion about something the author wishes to support. For expository articles, the title tells what specific explanatory information is about to be provided. A focused thesis statement helps determine what will be in the essay; the subsequent paragraphs are spent developing and supporting the central idea.

In addition to presenting the thesis statement, a well-written opening paragraph captures the attention of the reader and explains why the topic is important. It may provide the reader with background information on the subject matter. It may also preview what points will be covered in the following paragraphs.

The introduction is then followed by three (or more) supporting paragraphs. These are the main body of the essay. Each paragraph presents and develops a unique argument or clarification that supports or develops the thesis statement of the entire essay. The writer can use various kinds of supporting material and details to support the topics of each supporting paragraph. These may include statistics, quotations from people with special knowledge or expertise, historic facts, and anecdotes.

The conclusion is the paragraph that closes the essay. Also called the ending or summary paragraph, its function is to summarize or restate the main idea of the essay. It may recall an idea from the introduction or briefly examine the larger implications of the thesis.

Explaining the Cloning Process That Created Dolly

Editor's Notes This first model essay is a process, or how-to, essay that explains the procedure used to create Dolly, the first cloned sheep. As you read this essay, take note of the information provided and how it is organized and presented (the sidebar notes provide further information on the essay). In addition, consider the following questions:

1. How does the introduction engage the reader's attention?
2. What is the essay's general thesis?
3. What is done to help the reader transition from one paragraph to the next?

The first sentence gets the reader's attention by implicitly raising a question—what was so special about this sheep? The following sentences answer the question and introduce the essay's topic—cloning.

The concluding sentence of this paragraph serves as the thesis of the essay. The essay will be to explain how SCNT works and also examine why it is so difficult.

Brief definitions of somatic cells and genes are included in the second paragraph.

In 1997 a sheep made newspaper headlines around the world. What made Dolly, born at the Roslin Institute in Scotland in July 1996, special was the way she was created. Dolly had no biological father or mother. She was the first mammal to be cloned from an adult cell. The cloning method that scientists Ian Wilmut and Keith Campbell used to make her is called somatic cell nuclear transfer (SCNT), a procedure that is simple to explain but difficult to carry out in practice.

The challenge facing Wilmut and Campbell was to get an adult cell of a sheep to begin the process of dividing and subdividing into a whole new sheep. All adult somatic cells (that is, all cells except for eggs and sperm) contain within them all the genes necessary to create an entire organism. These genes are special chemicals that serve as biological blueprints. In nature, these cells only use their genes to begin the development process to create a new organism after the male sperm and female egg combine. The fertilized egg then follows its genetic instructions and starts dividing into many cells. At some point the cells start specializing into nerve, brain, muscle, and other cells; the ultimate result is a new organism. These somatic cells contain in their nucleus the same full genetic information that is used to guide the fertilized egg's development into a new being. However, these specialized adult cells have had most of their chemical instructions turned off. Molecular biologist Larisa Rudenko says that their nucleus "has matured to a point where its instructions are 'locked away' in a configuration specific to the job that the cell is intended to perform." To clone a new organism using the material in somatic cells, these genetic instructions have to be reactivated—a process called epigenetic reprogramming.

To reprogram an adult sheep cell, Wilmut and Campbell combined it with an egg cell. They first took an adult somatic cell from a female sheep and put it in a state of hibernation by starving it of nutrients. They took an egg cell, or oocyte, from another female adult sheep and carefully removed its genetic material. The resulting egg cell retained nutrients and cellular machinery necessary for development. The scientists then combined the prepared somatic cell and the prepared egg cell by fusing them with electricity. The newly combined cell began to divide as in sexual fertilization. The cell division resulted in an embryo that was cultivated in a laboratory and then implanted into the uterus of a third female sheep. The final result after gestation and delivery was a lamb that was virtually genetically identical to the female sheep that contributed the somatic cell.

The actual process of carrying out all of these steps is far from foolproof. In fact, the researchers who made Dolly used SCNT on 277 oocytes. Of these, only 29 successfully fused into developing embryos that could be implanted into female sheep. And of those, Dolly was the only one to be successfully born. Similar low success rates have been found in other animal cloning experiments, with many cloned animals dying in utero or

The exposition leads into two fundamental points about somatic cells: 1) they have all the original genetic instructions, and 2) these instructions have been "locked away." A quotation from a scientific authority restates and elaborates upon these points and the problem they pose—how to "reprogram" the genetic instructions.

Definitions of technical terms are often helpful in expository writing about complex subjects.

The paragraph's opening (and thesis) sentence explains how the challenge raised in the prior paragraph is met.

The following sentences lend support to the paragraph's thesis by providing sequential, step-by-step details on the solution.

The first sentence serves as the paragraph's thesis; it supports the second part of the essay's overall thesis.

Concrete examples are given of how SCNT is not a foolproof process.

exhibiting health problems after birth. Scientists have several explanations for the low success rates. The SCNT process of removing and replacing nuclei creates stress on both the egg and the somatic cells. In addition, much uncertainty still exists as to how to induce cells to successfully undertake epigenetic reprogramming—getting the adult stem cell nucleus to successfully reactivate all its genetic instructions and behave like an embryonic cell.

As for Dolly herself, the famous sheep remained at the institute where she was born and gave birth to several (uncloned) lambs. She was euthanized in 2003 at the age of six after suffering from arthritis and a progressive lung disease—conditions usually found in older sheep. Her premature death has raised further questions about the long-term health effects of cloning. Dolly provided the world with living proof that cloning through SCNT was indeed possible, but she also helped to demonstrate that cloning was far from easy.

> Several possible reasons are given for the statistics described above. The central problem of epigenetic reprogramming is again stressed.

> The concluding paragraph refers to the sheep introduced at the essay's beginning.

> The last sentence restates the essay's thesis while underscoring Dolly's importance.

Exercise One — Create an Outline from an Existing Essay

In many cases it helps to create an outline of the five-paragraph essay before you write it. The outline can help you organize the information, arguments, and evidence you have gathered in your research.

In most five-paragraph essays, the introductory paragraph presents the thesis of the essay, and the conclusion restates the thesis. The middle three paragraphs present information that elaborates upon and supports the thesis. It is for this middle section that an outline can be especially helpful.

For this exercise, create an outline that could have been used to write the three supporting paragraphs of Essay One. This "reverse engineering" exercise is meant to help familiarize you with how outlines can help classify and arrange information.

Part of the outline has already been started to give you an idea of the assignment.

Outline
 I. Write the essay's thesis:
II. Paragraph Two
A. **Thesis** (the main point of the paragraph that supports the essay's thesis): The challenge facing Wilmut and Campbell was how to induce or "reprogram" an adult cell to subdivide and form a whole new organism (note: a problem requiring a solution).
B. **Supporting Evidence/Explanation**
1. Adult somatic cells contain all of the genes (chemical instructions) used to form an entire organism.
2. The only time in nature when all of these instructions are used to create a new organism is right after fertilization (combining of male sperm and female egg).
3. Following that initial development process, the cells of animals have become specialized and have had most of their genetic instructions "locked away."
4. An adult somatic cell thus needs _____.
III. Paragraph Three
A. **Thesis:** Wilmut and Campbell's solution to reprogramming an adult sheep cell was combining it with an egg cell.

B. Supporting Evidence/Explanation

    1. First step: taking an adult somatic cell from a female sheep.

    2.

    3.

    4.

IV. Paragraph 4

A. Thesis:

B. Supporting Evidence/Elaboration

    1. Only 29 out of 277 cloning attempts by Wilmut and Campbell became embryos.

    2.

    3.

    4.

Why Cloning for Embryonic Stem Cells Is So Controversial

Essay
Two

Editor's Notes The second essay, also written in five paragraphs, is an expository essay that provides information on embryonic stem cells and attempts to explain why they are the cause of political controversy. It explains the controversy over stem cells and describes the opposing positions people have taken on the issue, but, unlike a persuasive essay, it does not take sides on the dispute. Throughout the essay, information and direct quotations from other sources, including viewpoints in the previous section, are used to illustrate and support what the essay is attempting to explain.

As you read the essay, take note of the questions and notes on the side. These are meant to help you analyze how this essay is organized and written.

Some say they hold the key to medical miracles. Others assert that using them would create a slippery ethical slope in which humans are created and destroyed for their parts. They have played a central role in debates over whether to ban human cloning. What are they? Embryonic stem cells. These cells are at the center of a charged political hullabaloo in which both sides contend that human lives hang in the balance.

Human embryonic stem cells are cells that form very early in human development, before cells start to differentiate into specialized cells such as nerve and blood cells. They are pluripotent—that is, they have the potential to develop into different types of tissue, such as nerves, muscle, or skin. This capacity has caught the attention of medical researchers, especially after human stem cells were first isolated in a scientific laboratory at the University of Wisconsin in 1998. Scientists theorize

How is the topic of the essay introduced? Does it grab the reader's attention?

What is the thesis of the essay?

What is the purpose of this paragraph? Is the purpose explicitly laid out in one sentence?

Why is the word *pluripotent* worth defining in this instance?

75

that injecting such cells into patients whose own cells have been damaged or are aging may provide relief or even recovery from many degenerative diseases, such as Alzheimer's or Parkinson's disease. Some stem cell research advocates, such as writer David Holcberg, have gone even further in envisioning a future in which stem cells could be used to grow "healthy new skin for fire victims; . . . or new retinas for blind people; or new spinal cords for paraplegics."

From which page of this book is Holcberg's quotation taken?

Scientists have proposed using what they call therapeutic cloning to obtain supplies of embryonic stem cells necessary to research and develop the treatments that may make Holcberg's dreams a reality. This works by using a jolt of energy to fuse the genetic nucleus of a patient's own cell with an enucleated human egg cell. If successful, the combined cell begins the process of cellular division to produce an embryo (also called a blastocyst). Within two weeks, when the embryo consists of 100 to 150 cells, embryonic stem cells can then be taken from it and cultured in the laboratory. A possible and important benefit of stem cells produced by therapeutic cloning is that they share almost all of the same genes as the patient. Therefore, after they are injected into a patient's body, they may have a lower risk of being rejected as foreign invaders by the patient's immune system.

The paragraph's first sentence introduces cloning; the linkage back to Holcberg helps knit together the two paragraphs.

These sentences provide how-to information on how scientists want to use cloning to create stem cells.

However, some have argued that using cloning as a source of stem cells, even if it holds great medical promise, is morally wrong. The embryo dies when stem cells are extracted. While Holcberg flatly states that "a human embryo is not a human being," many people, especially those opposed to abortion, strongly believe that human life at this early stage should never be willfully destroyed. The process of creating and harvesting stem cells "actually produces a new, genetically complete human life for the sole purpose of destroying it," writes philosophy professor John Morris. "This simply cannot be tolerated in any civilized society." Such concerns for preserving

How is the transition to this paragraph handled?

embryonic life were at the forefront when 262 members of Congress in 2001 voted to criminalize all human cloning, including the cloning of embryos for stem cell extraction (the legislation died after the Senate failed to act on it).

Both sides of the embryonic stem cell debate claim to save lives. Holcberg argues that a therapeutic cloning ban would prevent scientists from developing effective medical treatments and thus "end up sacrificing real human beings for microscopic clusters of cells." But cloning opponents maintain that they are the ones preserving human life. "Our society needs to ban human cloning to prevent the creation and destruction of human life, whether embryonic or more advanced," argues bioethics professor and cloning opponent Donal P. O'Mathuna. The life-and-death stakes of this debate cited by people on both sides may make any political compromise on therapeutic cloning unlikely.

David Holcberg, "Therapeutic Cloning Is Pro-Life," *Capitalism Magazine*, December 19, 2001.

John Morris, "Stem Cell Research Will Offer No 'Advance' for Society," *Business Journal*, February 25, 2005.

Donal P. O'Mathuna, "Human Cloning, by Any Other Name, Should Be Banned," *Columbus Dispatch*, November 27, 2001.

> Sentences on Congress explain another connection between cloning and embryonic stem cells.

> Why should quotations be used to supply positions when writing an expository essay about a controversial issue?

> How does the concluding sentence both restate and expand upon the essay's thesis?

> This is an example of an informal listing of sources used for this essay. More discussion of how and when to cite sources can be found in Appendix B.

Exercise Two

Create an Expository Essay Outline Using Opposing Views

For this exercise, you will create a thesis and an outline for a five-paragraph expository essay based on a pair of opposing viewpoints in the previous section of this book.

Part 1: Essay Topic and Thesis
The titles of Viewpoints One and Two each present the thesis and topic of their respective persuasive essays.

Combining the two into one sentence can give you the topic and thesis for an expository essay, such as "Animal Cloning Brings Both Potential Benefits and Potential Risks" or "Progress in Animal Cloning Has Raised Concerns About Whether Its Risks Outweigh Its Rewards."

Part 2: Take Notes from Viewpoints One and Two
Given the topic you are focusing on, it might help to organize your notes by dividing them into different columns or categories, such as "The Risks of Animal Cloning," "The Rewards of Animal Cloning," "The Role of Government," and "Other Information."

Under each column, write down notes derived from the viewpoints. These could include the following:
- illustrations or specific examples (of risks or benefits of cloning)
- statistical information
- direct quotations from authorities or from article
- anecdotes of past events
- definitions of technical terms

Part 3: Topic Sentences
Write down three or more topic sentences that define and explain the thesis from Part 1. Beneath each sentence, write down the appropriate notes from Part 2 that support that topic sentence. Here's an example of a topic sentence: Animal cloning promises several benefits to farmers and consumers. Supporting information, taken from Viewpoint One would be as follows:
- Scientists and farmers are hoping the descendants of cloned animals will become sources of food and clothing and are awaiting FDA approval.
- Cloning can ensure that consumers get a great steak every time they order one at a restaurant.

- Cloning improves the ability of farmers to select and propagate the best and most productive animals, avoiding the "roulette wheel" of breeding.
- Full Flush, a prize grand champion bull, can't meet demand for his breeding services, but five new clones may help with that.

Part 4: Create an Outline

Thesis statement: Animal Cloning Brings Both Potential Benefits and Potential Risks

I. Supporting sentence: Animal Cloning Promises Several Benefits to Farmers and Consumers
  A. Details and elaboration
II. Supporting sentence 2
  A. Details and elaboration
III. Supporting sentence 3
  A. Details and elaboration

Part 5: Write the Arguments in Paragraph Form

You now have three arguments that support the paragraph's thesis statement as well as supporting material. Use the outline to write your three supporting arguments in paragraph form. Each paragraph has a topic sentence that states the paragraph's thesis and supporting sentences that express the facts, details, and examples that support the paragraph's argument. The paragraph may also have a concluding or summary sentence.

Analyzing and Writing the Introduction and Conclusion

The introductory and concluding paragraphs can greatly improve your expository essay by quickly identifying the essay's main idea for readers.

The Introduction

Well-written introductions not only present the essay's thesis or core idea, but they also grab the attention of readers and tell them why the topic is important and interesting. There are several techniques you can use in the opening paragraph to attract the reader's attention:

- Clearly state the essay's thesis.
- Use an anecdote: a brief newsworthy or historical story that illustrates a point relevant to the topic.
- Include startling information: true and pertinent facts or statistics that illustrate the point of the essay. A brief opening assertion can then be elaborated upon over the next few sentences.
- Raise a question: Begin the essay with a question or problem that the rest of the essay attempts to answer or resolve.
- Provide information: The first sentence or two introduces the topic in general terms, with each sentence becoming gradually more specific, until you conclude with your thesis statement.

Step 1: Reread the introductory paragraphs of the model essays and of the eight viewpoints of the previous section. Identify which of the techniques described above were used in each essay or viewpoint. How else do they get the attention of the reader while presenting the thesis statement of the essay?

Step 2: Write an introduction for the essay you have outlined and partially written for Exercise Two. You can use one of the techniques described above.

The Conclusion

The conclusion brings the essay to a close by summarizing or restating its main argument(s). Good conclusions go beyond simply repeating the argument, however. They also answer the reader's question of "so what?"—in other words, they tell why the argument is important to consider. Some conclusions may also explore the broader implications of the thesis argument. They may close with a quotation or refer back to an anecdote or event in the essay. In argumentative essays over controversial topics, the conclusion reiterates the essay's position. In expository essays that do not take sides, the conclusion may summarize the main points in contention.

Step 3: Reread the concluding paragraphs of the model essays and of the eight viewpoints of the previous section. Which were most effective in driving their arguments home to the reader? What sorts of devices did they use?

Step 4: Write a conclusion for the essay you have outlined and partially written in Exercise Two.

The Motivations Behind Animal and Human Cloning

Editor's Notes The following expository essay uses classification as an organizing principle. Its topic is the various motivations behind animal and human cloning research. It categorizes these motivations into utilitarian and noneconomic categories and examines how both kinds of motivations are behind animal and human cloning.

This essay, unlike the first two, is longer than five paragraphs. Sometimes five paragraphs are simply not enough to adequately develop an idea. Despite the greater length of the essay, it does not address some items. For example, there is no explanation of what cloning is or how it works; the writer is assuming that the reader already has such basic knowledge. There is also little discussion of whether cloning can in fact satisfy the motivations described in the essay. Attempting to cover too much can cause an essay to lose focus and unity. Instead, the paragraphs remain focused on the purpose of describing and categorizing the reasons people give to pursue cloning.

As you read this essay, consider the sidebar questions, including those asking to identify the essay's and paragraph's thesis statements.

The first two sentences introduce the general topic—cloning.

The 1997 news that a cloned sheep had been born moved the cloning of mammals from the realm of science fiction to reality. Since the birth of Dolly the sheep, scientists have succeeded in cloning calves, mice, cats, and other mammals, while others have conducted controversial research into human reproductive cloning. But cloning has remained not only a controversial process but also a very expensive one. A cloned farm animal costs about twenty thousand dollars to produce. People have paid even greater sums to scientists to pursue human cloning.

These sentences narrow the topic to the expense of cloning.

The willingness of people to pay such sums raises the question: Why are people so highly motivated to create new life with cloning rather than with the natural method of sexual reproduction? The answer to that question depends in part on what is being cloned. The motivations behind the cloning of Dolly the sheep and other farm animals fall into a different category than the motivations behind the cloning of pets, which in turn may differ from the motivation for cloning human babies. This essay will briefly examine the various categories of reasons for cloning.

The motivation behind cloning farm animals is economic. The ultimate goal of farmers is to maximize the utility of their animals. Farmers want animals with certain qualities. Ranchers want cattle that are resistant to disease and provide tasty, tender meat. Dairy farmers want cows that give lots of milk. Sheep farmers want their animals to produce lots of quality wool. All of these characteristics are controlled in part by an animal's genes. Farmers have used selective breeding to try to improve the genetic endowments of their animals, but this process is slow and the results uncertain. Cloning could enable farmers to guarantee that a genetically superior animal could be readily and accurately replicated. Law professor Sherry F. Colb writes that "cloning sheep would thus resemble the mass production of seedless oranges: genetic engineering designed to increase the pleasure and value humans get from property."[1]

The value of cloned animals can go beyond the harvesting of meat, milk, and wool. Animals have also been seen as a potential source for drugs and medical compounds. The private company that provided the research funding for the creation of Dolly was not necessarily interested in better wool, but rather in animals that could be genetically engineered to create human proteins and other medicines. Introducing human genes in animals is itself a very difficult feat; a successfully engineered animal would be extremely valuable and thus would be a prime candidate for cloning.

After the topic has been introduced, the second paragraph provides the thesis of the essay. What is the thesis?

How is the structure of the essay foreshadowed in this paragraph?

What is the purpose of the last sentence?

What is the topic sentence for this paragraph? How does it support the thesis of the essay?

This quotation uses an analogy to explain a point. A footnote provides the source (see Appendix B).

Is the first or second sentence in this paragraph the topic sentence within the structure of the essay?

How is a specific example of cloning, already mentioned in the essay's opening, used to support this paragraph's point?

1. Sherry F. Colb, "Why the Cloned Cat Makes the Case Against Human Cloning," Findlaw.com, February 27, 2002.

For medical researchers, it is the genetic sameness of clones that gives them economic value. Cloned mice and other laboratory animals can be tested for medicines or used in other experiments. Scientists testing two different drugs, for example, could study the differences in how they affect animals. If cloned animals were used, the researchers would have greater assurance that any differences observed would be because of the drugs, not because of genetic differences between different mice. Cloning would also avoid the problems of selective inbreeding. In the past, selective inbreeding was the only way to obtain a genetically uniform set of animals for experiments; however, it also created health problems for the inbred animals.

Such practical considerations had relatively little importance when the birth of a cloned cat (named Carbon Copy) was announced at Texas A&M University in 2001. The multimillion-dollar funding for that research was provided by John Sperling, a wealthy entrepreneur who wanted a clone of his dog (cats proved easier to clone). Sperling later founded a company named Genetic Savings & Clone (GSC), which has since cloned several cats at a cost of fifty thousand dollars each. The willingness of Sperling and other pet owners to part with such sums of money to clone their pets is more emotional than practical. They do not want to use cloning for mass production or to improve the genetics of herd animals; instead, their desire is to clone a beloved pet. They saw their pets not as a product but as beloved family members. Many pet owners whose pets have died seek to recapture the emotional bond or relationship they had with their animal. Some have paid hundreds of dollars to GSC to preserve a genetic sample of their dead cat or dog in the hopes that eventually they will be able to clone a replacement.

A similar emotional motivation lies behind some of the push for human reproductive cloning. In some tragic cases, parents who have seen their children die have come to believe that cloning may provide a way of filling the void left behind. Clonaid, a company formed by the religious group the Raelians to pursue human cloning, contends that its funding came from an anonymous couple whose ten-year-old son died in surgery. The grieving parents had saved cells from their child in the hope that a new boy could be cloned one day.

In addition to parents who have lost a child, many people want to have children of their own but are unable to have them naturally. These include people with fertility problems as well as single people and same-sex couples. Many already go through expensive and difficult assisted-reproduction treatments; cloning would provide another possible avenue of reproduction. The desire to have children—cloned or not—has both altruistic and selfish elements, but most would agree that it has little resemblance to the farmer's desire for more productive sheep and cattle.

This is not to say that utilitarian motivations for cloning children have not been contemplated. However, such ideas have usually been raised by opponents of cloning who believe that all cloning should be banned or restricted. Some critics raise the possibility that human clones could be mass produced to create armies (a scenario familiar to the fans of the Star Wars movies). Others point to the possibility that human clones could be created in order to donate their organs to the person from whom they were cloned. But proponents of cloning dismiss these warnings of exploiting human clones by noting that they would be unique individuals possessing equal human rights. "Laws already prohibit criminal masterminds from holding slaves, abusing children, or cutting up people for spare body parts," writes lawyer and human cloning advocate Mark D. Eibert, arguing that laws against human cloning are unnecessary.[2]

Understanding why some people want to pursue cloning at great cost, and distinguishing between the different types of motivations for cloning animals and humans, can help clarify and frame the ongoing moral and ethical debates over whether cloning should be banned, regulated, or permitted without restrictions. Many people believe that it is

> Here another specific example is provided to illustrate the general point of the paragraph.

> This sentence continues the comparison between human and animal cloning.

> Where is the thesis restated in the conclusion? What else does the conclusion do?

2. Mark D. Eibert, "Clone Wars," *Reason*, June 1998.

acceptable for humans to exploit animals for utilitarian purposes, and they may well extend this acceptance to the cloning of animals. Conversely, most people do not accept that humans have the right to exploit other humans for utilitarian or selfish purposes. But whether that means that all human cloning should be criminalized—even human cloning for infertile couples harboring the emotional desire to have a child of their own—remains in question. Regardless of how the debate over cloning turns out, the amount of money being spent on cloning suggests that many people will continue, from a variety of motivations, to pursue cloning no matter what governments decide.

Exercise
Four
Steps to Write Your Own Five-Paragraph Expository Essay

The final exercise is to write your own five-paragraph (or longer) expository essay that focuses on and explains something about cloning. You can use the resources in this book both for information about cloning and how to write and organize an expository essay.

Step 1: Decide on the Topic

For this exercise, the topic is cloning. However, cloning is too broad a subject for a short essay without becoming superficial. The first step is to narrow the topic so as to be able to write about it effectively in five paragraphs. One might use a triangle to illustrate the process.

For example, for Viewpoint Three of this book, the following triangle could illustrate the topic.

cloning

human cloning

the ethics of human cloning

the actions of Raelians and other irresponsible cloning advocates

George Dvorsky doesn't refer to animal cloning, therapeutic cloning of stem cells, or to laws governing cloning. He remains focused on the ethics of human cloning and on examining the differences between ethical and unethical cloning activities.

For Essay Three, the triangle could read:

cloning
reproductive cloning
motivations for reproductive cloning

For your exercise, fill in at least three triangles to come up with a limited topic for your cloning essay. Then pick one to continue on to the next step.

cloning
limited topic
limited topic
topic of essay

cloning

cloning

Some possible questions to help you decide on a topic:
- *Why is this topic important?*
- *Why should people be interested in this topic?*
- *What question am I going to answer in this paragraph or essay?*
- *How can I best answer this question?*
- *What facts or ideas can I use to support the answer to my question?*
- *How can I make this essay interesting to the reader?*

Step 2: Gather Facts and Ideas Related to Your Topic
This volume contains several places to find information, including the viewpoints and the appendices. In addition, you may want to research the books, articles, and Web sites listed in the bibliography, or do additional research in your local library.

If you are using direct quotations or statements from someone, it is usually important to note his or her qualifications and possible biases.

Step 3: Develop a Workable Thesis Statement
Use what you have written down in the above steps to help you choose the ideas you want to emphasize in your essay.

Remember that the thesis statement has two parts: the topic (whatever aspect of cloning you chose in Step 1) and the point of the essay. Through the thesis, you are announcing your topic to the reader, and stating what you believe is significant about that topic. The thesis helps organize and determine what information will be included in the essay. Here are two examples of thesis statements:
- Human cloning raises problems of family identity.
- Cloning is a controversial proposed method of preserving endangered species.

Step 4: Write an Outline or Diagram
To write an outline or diagram, follow these steps:
1. Write the thesis statement at the top.
2. Write roman numerals I, II, and III on the left side of the page.
3. Next to each roman numeral, write down the best arguments/elaborations/examples you have written down from Step 3. These should all directly relate to and support the thesis statement. If the essay is a problem/solution essay, write down the problem and the solution. If it is a process or how-to essay, write the sequence of steps. If it is a classification essay, write down the categories being analyzed.

4. Under each roman numeral, write a capital letter (A, B, C, etc.). Next to each letter, write down facts or information that support that roman numeral's idea.
5. An alternative to the roman numeral outline is the diagram (see box).

Diagrams—an Alternative to Outlines

Although many students prefer to use a roman numeral outline, an alternative method of organizing ideas on paper is the diagram. A possible approach would go as follows:

1. Draw a circle in the middle of the page. In that circle, write the topic of the essay.
2. Draw three or four lines out from the circle. Draw an additional circle at the end of each line.
3. In each circle, write some arguments or points about the topic.
4. Draw three or four lines out of each outer circle and place circles at the ends of those lines.
5. In each new circle, write some facts or information that support that particular idea.

Step 5: Write the Three Supporting Paragraphs

Use your outline or diagram to write the three supporting paragraphs. Write down the main point in sentence form. Do the same for the supporting points of information. Each sentence should support the topic of the paragraph. Sometimes (not always), paragraphs include a conclusion or summary sentence that restates the paragraph's argument.

Step 6: Write the Introduction and Conclusion

See Exercise Three for information on writing introductions and conclusions.

Step 7: Read and Rewrite

After you have written your rough draft, it is important to reread your essay. Ask yourself the following questions during your review:

- Does the essay maintain a consistent tone?
- Do all sentences reinforce your general thesis?
- Do paragraphs flow from one to the other? Do you need transition words or phrases?
- Is there a sense of progression—does each paragraph advance the argument by offering more information than preceding paragraphs?
- Are there any spelling or grammatical errors?
- Does the essay get bogged down in too much detail or irrelevant material?

Tips on Writing Effective Essays

- Write in the active, not passive, voice.
- Vary your sentence structure, especially in stating and restating your thesis.
- Maintain a professional, reasonable tone of voice. Avoid sounding too uncertain or insulting.
- Use sources that state facts and evidence.
- Do not write in the first person.
- Avoid assumptions or generalizations without evidence.

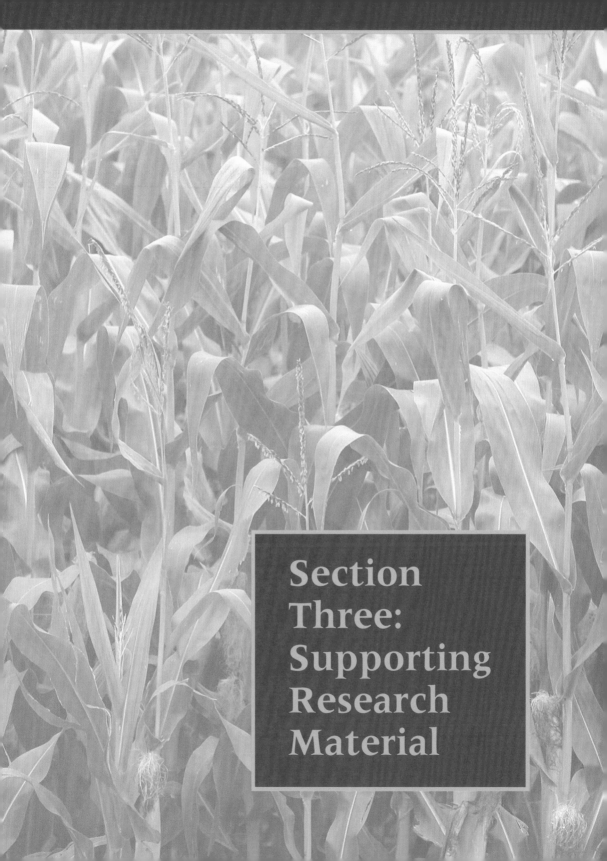

Section Three: Supporting Research Material

Facts About Cloning

Editor's Note: These facts can be used in reports or papers to reinforce or add credibility when making important points or claims.

Cloning Science

- Contrary to depictions in movies, cloning does not create instant carbon copies of adults.
- Animals created with the SCNT process are almost, but not quite, a complete genetic match with the donor animal. The clone shares the donor's nuclear DNA, but a small amount of the cloned animal's genes come from the mitochondria in the enucleated egg.
- In addition to slight genetic differences, cloned animals differ in how their genes may express themselves and in the environment in which they are raised.
- Mammals that have been cloned from adult cells since Dolly the sheep include mice, cattle, goats, monkeys, pigs, and cats.
- The success rate for animal cloning experiments has ranged from 0.1 percent to 3 percent, which means that for every one thousand tries, only one to thirty clones are made.
- About 30 percent of mammal clones born alive are affected with large offspring syndrome and other debilitating conditions.
- Cloned animals tend to have more compromised immune function and higher rates of infection, tumor growth, and other disorders than noncloned animals.
- In 2002 researchers at the Whitehead Institute for Biomedical Research in Cambridge, Massachusetts, reported that their analysis of more than ten thousand liver and placenta cells of cloned mice found that about 4 percent of genes functioned abnormally.
- Another question people have raised about clones is premature aging. As cells divide, the DNA sequences

at both ends of a cell's chromosome, called telomeres, shrink in length. Some scientists have theorized that if the transferred nucleus in a cloned animal is already old its shortened telomeres may affect the clone's life span. Scientists examining this phenomenon have found conflicting results. Dolly the sheep's chromosomes had shorter telomere lengths than normal. On the other hand, chromosomes from cloned cattle or mice had longer telomeres than normal. To date, scientists aren't sure why cloned animals show differences in telomere length.

Human Cloning Claims and Facts

- In the 1978 book *In His Image: The Cloning of a Man*, author David Rorvik purported to tell the story of an aging millionaire who created a clone of himself to inherit his wealth. The publisher later admitted the story to be a hoax.
- In 1997 a Chicago physicist, Richard Seed, announced plans to start work on cloning a human being.
- In December 2002 Clonaid, the organization affiliated with the Raelian religious cult, announced that a cloned baby girl named Eve had been born on December 26, 2002. Clonaid said other births were forthcoming. However, no genetic tests were ever held to confirm that a clone had in fact been born.
- In September 2003 Dr. Panos Zavos claimed to have created the world's first cloned human embryo. In January 2004 he announced that a thirty-five-year-old woman was set to give birth to the world's first cloned baby. Neither story has been verified.
- In February 2004 researchers in South Korea announced they had successfully cloned thirty human embryos and had extracted stem cells from one of them.
- In February 2005 Ian Wilmut, the creator of Dolly the sheep, received a license to clone human embryos using cells from people with a deadly neurological disease with the aim of studying how the disease progresses. Wilmut has opposed reproductive cloning, however.

Laws

- The UN General Assembly voted 84 to 34 on March 8, 2005, to adopt a declaration calling on governments to ban all forms of human cloning that are "incompatible with human dignity and the protection of human life." The resolution is not legally binding. Nations that voted in favor of the ban include Australia, Bolivia, Costa Rica, Ethiopia, Germany, Hungary, Iraq, Ireland, Italy, Mexico, Nicaragua, the Philippines, Poland, Portugal, Rwanda, Saudi Arabia, Switzerland, Tajikistan, and the United States. Nations opposed include Belgium, Brazil, Cambodia, Canada, China, Cuba, the Democratic People's Republic of Korea, Denmark, Estonia, Finland, France, India, Jamaica, Japan, the Netherlands, New Zealand, Norway, the Republic of Korea, Singapore, Spain, Sweden, and the United Kingdom.
- In 2000 Britain became the first country to grant a patent for cloned human embryos; the corporation receiving the patent said it had no intention of creating cloned humans.
- The American Medical Association and the American Association for the Advancement of Science have both issued formal statements advising against human reproductive cloning.
- As of July 2004, only 30 of the 191 states recognized by the United Nations have passed laws banning human reproductive cloning. These include Great Britain, Belgium, Canada, Denmark, Germany, the Netherlands, and Spain.
- As of 2005 the United States has no federal law against reproductive cloning.
- In 1997 California became the first state to pass legislation against human reproductive cloning. Since then eight other states—Arkansas, Iowa, Michigan, Rhode Island, North Dakota, Virginia, New Jersey, and South Dakota—have passed laws banning cloning. Of these nine states, five—Arkansas, Iowa, Michigan, North Dakota, and South Dakota—extend their legal ban on cloning to include research or therapeutic cloning (cloning to create embryos for stem cell and other research).

Finding and Using Sources of Information

Expository writing is writing that imparts information. This information often comes from other sources, such as books, magazine articles, and online articles. This appendix provides some basic information on how to find and use information sources when writing your expository essay.

Using Books and Articles

You can find books and articles in a library by using the library's cataloging system. You can also use a computer to find many magazine articles and other articles written specifically for the Internet.

You are likely to find a lot more information than you can possibly use in your essay, so your first task is to narrow it down to what is likely to be most usable. Look at book and article titles. Look at book chapter titles, and take a look at the book index to see if the book contains information on the specific topic you want to write about. (For example, if you want to write about the cloning of pets and you find a book about cloning, check the chapter titles and index to be sure it contains information about pet cloning before you bother to check it out.)

For a five-paragraph essay, you don't need a great deal of supporting information, so quickly try to narrow down your materials to a few good books and magazine or Internet articles. You don't need dozens. You might even find that one or two good books or articles contain all of the information you need.

You probably don't have time to read an entire book, so find the chapters or sections that relate to your topic, and skim these. When you find useful information, copy it onto a notecard or in a notebook. You should look for supporting facts, statistics, quotations, and examples.

Evaluate the Source

When you select your supporting information, it is important that you evaluate its source. This is especially important with information you find on the Internet. Because nearly anyone can put information on the Internet, there is as much bad information as there is good information. Before using Internet information—or any information—try to determine if the source seems reliable. Is the author or Internet site sponsored by a legitimate organization? Is it from a government source? Does the author have any special knowledge or training relating to the topic you are researching? Does the article give any indication of the origin of its information?

Using Your Supporting Information

When you use supporting information from a book, article, or other source, there are three important things to remember:

1. *Make it clear whether you are using a direct quotation or a paraphrase.* If you copy information directly from your source you are quoting it. You must put quotation marks around the information and identify the information's source. If you put the information in your own words, you are paraphrasing it.

Here is an example of using a quotation:

California attorney Mark D. Eibert raises serious questions on how a ban on human reproductive cloning would be enforced and what the FBI may have to do to investigate violations. "Would they raid research laboratories and universities? Seize and read the private medical records of infertility patients? Burst into operating rooms with their guns drawn? Grill new mothers about how their babies were conceived?"[1]

1. Mark D. Eibert, "Clone Wars," *Reason*, June 1998.

Here is an example of a brief paraphrase of the same passage:

California attorney Mark D. Eibert suggests that FBI agents may have to go after the private records of research laboratories and infertility patients or perhaps even grill new mothers right after their babies were born if a ban on human reproductive cloning was to be strictly enforced.

2. *Use the information fairly.* Be careful to use supporting information in the way the author intended it. There is a joke that movie ads containing critics' comments like "First-class!" "Best ever!" and other glowing phrases take them from longer reviews that said something like "This movie is first-class trash" or "This movie is this director's best ever—and that isn't saying much!" This is called taking information out of context (using it in a way the original writer did not intend). This is using supporting evidence unfairly.

3. *Give credit where credit is due.* You must give credit when you use someone else's information, but not every piece of supporting information needs a credit.

- If the supporting information is general knowledge—that is, it can be found in many sources—you do not have to cite (give credit to) your source.
- If you directly quote a source, you must give credit.
- If you paraphrase information from a specific source, you must give credit.
- If you do not give credit where you should, you are *plagiarizing*—or stealing—someone else's work.

There are a number of ways to give credit. Your teacher will probably want you to do it one of three ways:

- Informal: You tell where you got the information in the same place you use it.
- Informal list: At the end of the article, place an unnumbered list of the sources you used. This tells the reader where, in general, you got your information, but it doesn't tell specifically where you got any single fact.

- Formal: Use a footnote, like the first example in number 1 above. (A footnote is generally placed at the end of an article or essay, although it may be located in different places depending on your teacher's requirements.)

Be sure you know exactly what information your teacher requires before you start looking for your supporting information so that you know what information to include with your notes.

Sample Essay Topics

Definition Essays
What Is Cloning?
What Is a Clone?
Cloning May Change What It Means to Be Human

Classification Essays
Human Cloning Has Many Potential Benefits for Society
Human Cloning Has Many Potential Dangers for Society
Animal Cloning Has Many Benefits for Humans and Animals
Animal Cloning Has Potential Harms for Humans and Animals
The World's Religions Have Different Moral Rules on Cloning

Problem/Solution Essays
Cloning Can Help Couples Who Cannot Have Children Naturally
A Cloning Ban Would Prevent Dangerous Experiments in Human Cloning
Cloning Can Help Restore Children to Grieving Parents
Cloning Cannot Help Restore Children to Grieving Parents
Cloning Can Help Preserve Endangered Species

Persuasive Essays
All Forms of Human Cloning Should Be Banned
Reproductive, Not Therapeutic, Cloning Should Be Banned
Therapeutic, Not Reproductive, Cloning Should Be Banned
Research Cloning Is More Ethical than Reproductive Cloning
Reproductive Cloning Is More Ethical than Research Cloning
Human Cloning Is a Reproductive Right

Glossary

blastocyst: A fertilized egg in the early stages of development that consists of a ball of about 30 to 150 cells. The inner mass of cells will become the fetus, and the outer ring of cells will become part of the placenta, which envelopes the fetus and is attached to the mother's womb.

chromosomes: Long pieces of DNA located inside the nucleus of a cell that are duplicated each time the cell divides. Chromosomes transmit the genes of an organism from one generation to the next.

clone: 1) An exact genetic replica of a DNA molecule, cell, tissue, organ, or entire plant or animal. 2) An organism that has the same genetic makeup as another organism.

cloned embryo: An embryo that has been created by somatic cell nuclear transfer (SCNT) rather than by the union of a sperm and an egg. SCNT involves inserting the nucleus of a body cell into an egg from which the nucleus has been removed. The egg is then stimulated to develop into an embryo.

cloning: The process of creating a living organism or embryo that has the same genetic composition as an already existing or previously existing individual.

cytoplasm: The contents of a cell other than the nucleus. Cytoplasm consists of a fluid that contains structures known as organelles that carry out the functions of the cell.

differentiation: In cells, the process of changing from the kind of cell that can develop into any part of the body, called an undifferentiated cell, to a specialized cell such as a blood, nerve, or muscle cell.

DNA: A chemical, deoxyribonucleic acid, found primarily in the nucleus of cells. DNA is the genetic material that contains the instructions for making all the structures and materials the body needs to function. Chromosomes and their subunits, genes, are made up primarily of DNA.

embryo: The developing organism from the time of fertilization until a significant number of cells have specialized into body tissue cells and when the organism then becomes known as a fetus.

embryonic stem cells: The cells of an embryo that have not yet received the chemical signal to become specialized cells. These cells are called pluripotent because they have the potential to become a wide variety of specialized cell types.

embryo splitting or "twinning": The separation of an early-stage embryo into two or more embryos with identical genetic makeup, essentially creating identical twins, triplets, quadruplets, etc.

enucleated egg: An egg cell whose nucleus has been removed or destroyed.

eugenics: An attempt to alter the genetic constitution of future generations with the aim of improving it.

gamete: A reproductive cell such as an egg or a sperm cell that has only one-half of the chromosomes needed to form an organism.

gene: A genetic unit of DNA located at a specific site on a chromosome.

genome: The complete genetic material of an organism.

germ cell or "germ line cell": Reproductive cells such as a sperm, an egg, or a cell that can develop into a sperm or an egg; all other body cells are called somatic cells.

in vitro fertilization: The fertilization of an egg by a sperm in an artificial environment outside the body. The term in vitro means, literally, "in glass": in a test tube, for example.

mitochondria: Cellular organs called organelles that provide the energy the cell needs to live. They contain some genetic material, the genetic information needed to keep the cell going, and enzymes that convert food into energy.

multipotent cell: A cell that can produce several different types of differentiated cells, which are cells that perform a specific function in the body such as blood, nerve, or muscle cells.

nuclear transfer: A procedure in which the nucleus from a donor cell is transferred into an egg from which the nucleus has been removed. The donor nucleus can come from a germ (reproductive) cell or a somatic (body) cell.

nucleus: A cellular organ that contains all of the cell's genes except those found in the mitochondria, the energy-producing organs of the cell.

oocyte: The developing female reproductive cell (the developing egg) that is produced in a female organism's ovaries.

organism: Any living individual considered as a whole.

pluripotent: A cell that can give rise to many different types of specialized cells.

somatic cell: All cells that are not reproductive (sperm or egg) cells. Somatic (body) cells have a complete set of chromosomes while reproductive cells have only half of a set.

somatic cell nuclear transfer (SCNT): The transfer of the nucleus from a donor somatic (body) cell into an egg from which the nucleus has been removed in order to produce a cloned embryo.

stem cells: Undifferentiated cells that can replicate indefinitely and which can differentiate and produce other specialized cells. They are found in embryos, umbilical cords, and adult body tissues.

totipotent: A cell that can develop into any kind of cell, which in turn develop into a complete adult organism and its tissues.

Organizations to Contact

The Center for Bioethics and Human Dignity
2065 Half Day Rd., Bannockburn, IL 60015
(847) 317-8180 • e-mail: info@cbhd.org
Web site: www.cbhd.org

The Center for Bioethics and Human Dignity is an international education center whose purpose is to bring Christian perspectives to bear on contemporary bioethical challenges facing society.

Clone Rights United Front/Clone Rights Action Center
506 Hudson St., New York, NY 10014
(212) 255-1439 • e-mail: r.wicker@verizon.net
Web site: www.clonerights.org

The Clone Rights United Front was organized to oppose legislation that would make cloning a human being a felony.

Genetic Savings & Clone, Inc. (GSC)
(888) 833-6063 • Web site: www.savingsandclone.com

GSC is a company that provides the commercial cloning of pets. Its Web site includes articles about cloning, its social benefits, and bioethical implications.

National Institutes of Health (NIH)
9000 Rockville Pike, Bethesda, MD 20892
(301) 4496-4000 • Web site: www.stemcells.nih.gov

The NIH is the federal government agency responsible for developing guidelines for research on stem cells.

People for the Ethical Treatment of Animals (PETA)
501 Front St., Norfolk, VA 23510 • (757) 622-7382
Web site: www.peta-online.org

PETA is an educational and activist group that opposes all forms of animal exploitation, including cloning.

President's Council on Bioethics
1801 Pennsylvania Ave. NW, Suite 700, Washington, DC 20006 • (202) 296-4669 • e-mail: info@bioethics.gov Web site: www.bioethics.gov

The council was formed by an executive order in 2001 to advise the president on bioethical issues raised by cloning and other emerging biotechnologies.

Web Sites

Americans to Ban Cloning (ABC) (www.cloning information.org)

ABC is a coalition of organizations and individuals whose goal is to promote a comprehensive, global ban on cloning. The Web site offers a variety of articles, commentaries, and congressional testimony against human cloning.

BetterHumans.com (www.betterhumans.com)

BetterHumans.com explores and advocates the use of science and technology to further human progress. The Web site's cloning link includes articles and commentary on cloning.

Clonaid (www.clonaid.com)

Clonaid was founded in 1997 by Rael, the spiritual leader of the Raelian movement. Clonaid is the first company to publicly announce its attempt to clone human beings.

The Clone Zone (www.bbc.co.uk/science/genes/gene_safari/clone_zone/intro.shtml)

A British Broadcasting Company Web site, the Clone Zone tells the history and science of cloning, with articles on human, pet, agricultural, animal, and endangered species cloning.

Cloning Fact Sheet (www.ornl.gov/sci/techresources/ Human_Genome/elsi/cloning.shtml)

This Web site is the creation of the Human Genome Project, a joint project coordinated by the U.S. Department of Energy and the National Institutes of Health. It includes background information on cloning and links to other Web sites.

Cloning in Focus (http://gslc.genetics.utah.edu/units/ cloning)

This Web site is the creation of the Genetic Science Learning Center, an outreach education program at the University of Utah. The Web site provides interactive and print-based resources that explore the science and ethics of cloning.

Human Cloning Foundation (www.humancloning.org)

The foundation promotes education, awareness, and research about human cloning and other forms of biotechnology.

Reproductive Cloning Network (www.reproductive cloning.net)

The Reproductive Cloning Network provides information on reproductive and therapeutic human cloning.

Bibliography

Books

Lori B. Andrews, *The Clone Age: Adventures in the New World of Reproductive Technology.* New York: Henry Holt, 1999.

Holly Cefrey, *Cloning and Genetic Engineering.* Danbury, CT: Childrens, 2002.

David Goodnough, *The Debate over Human Cloning.* Berkeley Heights, NJ: Enslow, 2003.

John Harris, *On Cloning.* London: Routledge, 2004.

Nancy Harris, ed., *Cloning.* San Diego: Greenhaven, 2005.

Leon R. Kass et al., *Human Cloning and Human Dignity: The Report of the President's Council on Bioethics.* New York: Public Affairs, 2002.

Arlene Judith Klotzko, *The Cloning Sourcebook.* New York: Oxford University Press, 2001.

Jane Maienschein, *Whose View of Life? Embryos, Cloning, and Stem Cells.* Cambridge, MA: Harvard University Press, 2003.

Glenn McGee, ed., *The Human Cloning Debate.* Berkeley, CA: Berkeley Hills, 2002.

Don Nardo, *Cloning.* San Diego: Lucent, 2005.

Martha C. Nussbaum and Cass R. Sunstein, *Clones and Clones: Facts and Fantasies About Human Cloning.* New York: Norton, 1998.

Gregory E. Pence, ed., *Flesh of My Flesh: The Ethics of Cloning Humans, a Reader.* Lanham, MD: Rowman & Littlefield, 1998.

Lee M. Silver, *Remaking Eden: Cloning and Beyond in a Brave New World.* New York: Avon, 1997.

Brent Waters and Ronald Cole-Turner, *God and the Embryo: Religious Voices on Stem Cells and Cloning.* Washington, DC: Georgetown University Press, 2003.

Ian Wilmut, Keith Campbell, and Colin Tudge, *The Second Creation: Dolly and the Age of Biological Control.* New York: Farrar, Straus and Giroux, 2000.

Periodicals

Ronald Bailey, "Is Brave New World Inevitable? Bill Kristol Says Yes. He's Wrong," *Reason,* April 24, 2002.

Hilary Bok, "Cloning Companion Animals Is Wrong," *Journal of Applied Animal Welfare Science,* 2002.

Thomas W. Clark, "Playing God, Carefully," *Humanist,* May 2000.

Kyla Dunn, "Cloning Trevor," *Atlantic,* June 2002.

Justine Durrell, "Can the Law Handle Human Cloning?" *Trial,* October 2002.

Economist, "Copy or Counterfeit?" January 4, 2003.

Thomas Fields-Meyer and Debbie Seaman, "Send in the Clones," *People,* September 8, 2003.

David van Gend, "The First Clone: Nobody's Child," *Human Life Review,* Fall 2001.

Brian Hanson, "Cloning Debate," *CQ Researcher,* October 22, 2004.

Rudolf Jaenisch and Ian Wilmut, "Don't Clone Humans!" *Science,* March 30, 2001.

Leon R. Kass, "The Public's Stake," *Public Interest,* Winter 2003.

Daniel J. Kevles, "Cloning Can't Be Stopped," *Technology Review,* June 1, 2002.

Charles Krauthammer, "The Fatal Promise of Cloning: Advocates Say They Will Never Create Human Fetuses. Can We Believe Them?" *Time,* June 24, 2002.

Chris Mooney, "The Future Is Later: The Cloning Fight Comes Down to Abortion—and Down to Earth," *American Prospect,* July 15, 2002.

Charles Murtaugh, "Shun Cloning: Scientists Must Speak Out," *Commonweal,* May 18, 2001.

Jeremy Rifkin, "Why I Oppose Human Cloning," *Tikkun,* July/August 2002.

Thomas A. Shannon, "The Rush to Clone: It Is Unethical to Apply This Unproven Research to Humans," *America,* September 10, 2001.

James Q. Wilson and Leon Kass, "The Ethics of Human Cloning," *American Enterprise,* March 1999.

Index

Picture Credits

About the Editor

William Dudley received his B.A. degree from Beloit College in Wisconsin, where he majored in English composition and wrote for the school newspaper and literary journal. He has since written and published op-ed pieces, travel articles, and other pieces of writing. He has edited dozens of books on history and social issues for Greenhaven Press at Thomson/Gale.